CYCLES (of) INTUITION

A journey of insights–

An inspiring story about business and life

Written and Illustrated by

I. Kostika

www.cyclesofintuition.com

For Hanna, in loving memory

Acknowledgements

To my children—Tzeela, Shira, Roey, Daphne and Johnathan, for their love, patience, support and advice throughout the writing of this book; and especially to Shira for her creative critique, and persistence for uncompromised quality.

To my business partner and close friend Yaron Lew for his ongoing support and involvement. His contribution and germination of ideas were vital in shaping this book.

Special thanks to my loyal friend Sally Shaw who spent many hours of reviewing and editing the story. Her unique skills and devotion were essential for the cohesiveness of this book.

To my special friend Jacob Vistanetzky for his interest and moral support.

To Ariel Zuhovitzky for his constructive comments; and other friends and colleagues for their help.

If there is anyone I have omitted to mention, please forgive me—I truly value everything you have contributed.

Contents

Preface

The carpenter does not call back, the flooring consultant disappears, the heating oil company responds weeks late to clean a semi-clogged burner nozzle, and at a retail store, a customer is wandering around helplessly looking for assistance.

I wonder, does it happen only to me?

But everybody else seems to experience similar incidents.

Don't they want my business? Are they so busy? Maybe they don't like me? How can this be when there is a recession? And if the economy is strong, don't they want more work? It all seems so contradictory.

What is going on? What is really missing?

When you are at work, you are in essence a service provider, no matter what you do. Even if you don't sell goods or services, just being at work and interacting with a co-worker or another department in your organization, puts you in that position—providing service to other people. The moment you leave work and look to buy something, you become a customer. It is amazing how quickly we change roles.

It seems that as a customer your view is totally different from that of a service provider; and as a provider too often your customer requirements are not met. Why is there such a dichotomy?

Reading this book will not only tell you why this happens, but help you discover what you must change. It will help you improve and grow—and make you prosper.

And if you elevate it to the personal and social interaction—from all walks of life—you will be able to gain from it all.

THE BEGINNING

This story begins with a phone call.

I was sitting at my desk in the office one evening after having a hectic day. The phone rang and I answered only to have one of the oddest conversations of my life.

On the other end of the line was a person who introduced himself as Steve, and Steve had a question which seemed to me peculiar.

"I am not sure why I am calling you, but I do hope you will be able to help me," he said.

I thought to myself, "How do I respond to that?" It was definitely not the type of question you encounter every day.

While my mind was working to come up with something, Steve added, "I'm a business owner and my business is doing well—very well compared to others in almost every aspect, and especially the bottom line."

Now my mind was working at full speed. Not only was it an unusual question, but deep inside I knew that I had to come up with something unique, and it had better be quick.

"Steve, I believe that being successful as you are, you wouldn't have taken the time and the effort to seek advice unless there was something out there bothering you. Probably your intuition is telling you that something is missing. Perhaps you sense that the answer is hidden beneath the surface."

There was a short silence and I could sense a slight hesitation. "That's a good point!" Steve responded. "So let me tell you about myself."

Then he began telling his story.

REWRITING THE BASICS

Old Traditions

"I was born and raised in a small town in the heartland of America," Steve said. "But this story isn't really about me—it's about Dad.

"Dad founded his company many years ago specializing in tool repair. His ability to restore tools even with the most complex technical challenges made his reputation very strong. He was regarded by many of his customers as a craftsman and managed to gain customers not only from our town but from the whole county.

"During my high school years, I had to help my father in the small family shop every day after school. I had to do all the low-level work: cleaning the floor, moving stuff around, filling shipment forms, helping with the loading and unloading of Dad's old pickup truck, and whatnot. It helped to save costs and off-load some pressure from my Dad's back."

Steve paused. "I guess Dad hoped that having me as his older son involved in the shop would, in the course of time, ensure that I carry on the family business after he retired."

Steve eventually left home for college. A few years later, right after graduation, he came back to his hometown to work for his dad in their small service shop—sometimes investing in our children's upbringing and education pays off.

Loaded with fresh ideas, Steve was hoping to immediately take the lead in the tiny business. But to his disappointment, his father put him right back to the tasks he was frustrated doing during high school, except this time it was for a full day's work with a small salary. Dad's belief was, "You learn everything from the bottom, and you can do it better now with full-time capacity. Slowly you will learn all business aspects and then you will work your way up." In those days this was an old tradition of a small town in America—especially for young people at the start of their careers.

Unlike many of his college graduate friends, Steve elected to give up an opportunity of a promising career in a large corporation to work in his father's shop, and he was getting frustrated. As a young business school grad he had much greater aspirations and was really getting ready to quit. However, for reasons he could not put his finger on, he stayed.

Perhaps Dad's way of hands-on education and deeply engrained family values kept Steve around. Maybe it was Steve's appreciation for Dad, who pushed him to go to college—which was not common in those days, and Dad was taking the risk that Steve might not be coming back. It may have been the entrepreneurial spirit and intuition that was telling Steve to stay.

Or maybe it was simply Steve's love for Sharon—his high school sweetheart—that kept him sticking around.

The Merits of Asking Why

"Dad's small shop was made up of some basic equipment, a few loyal employees, and technical manuals to help us keep our work to the highest standards. In most cases, it was even higher than our customers' requests," Steve eagerly continued his story.

"Frequently Dad would say to me, 'Give your customers the best quality around and they will come back again and again instead of going to your competition.' It was his number one principle for running the business, one that he would never compromise on."

A couple of years went by, and Steve's decision to tie his future with Dad changed his perspective of Dad's lifetime endeavor. Everything he used to do as a young kid and everything he had done since he came back from college, took on a different meaning—especially with the new responsibility and the outlook of a future business partner.

With this new view, Steve started analyzing everything according to the value it could bring to the business. After all, that was one of the very basic elements for business success that he had studied in college. No longer did he view cleaning the floor as an unpleasant chore. Now it was something necessary to keep up the high quality of work being performed in the shop. The same was true for carrying loads from Dad's old pickup, or filling shipping documents and preparing invoices. He even tried his hand at fixing a few tools with Dad's guidance. This turned out so badly that Dad had to put in three times more work than normal in order to salvage the tools.

Steve's failure in fixing tools did not dampen his vibrant spirit. He knew that over time, with Dad's guidance and some help from their loyal employees, he eventually would achieve the necessary knowledge. But Steve who was a young and dynamic person, although not a most technically capable one, owned another unique quality—the courage to ask questions about everything he did not fully understand.

Whether it was embedded in his nature or something he learned through his upbringing, he always had the question "Why?" pop up in his mind. At that time he did not realize how important it was, yet he would soon discover how it could change the course of things to come.

Steve was neither shy nor stupid, and he succeeded in irritating his Dad all too often. He always wanted to know how something they did could help and what value it could truly bring; and he often brought up to Dad suggestions for improvement.

Maybe it is the advantage someone has when he is young, fresh, and unafraid to question, and it doesn't hurt to be the owner's son....

Their frequent elaborate debates eventually helped Dad and Steve become closer as partners and friends. They put old generation barriers aside and found solutions to questions not usually asked, which in turn, eventually led to some improvements.

As time passed, it seemed that Steve was on track with Dad's plan to slowly groom him to become the future leader of their small enterprise. But little did Steve know that things were about to change, and change in a hurry.

Forgotten Values

3:00 p.m.

On one hectic afternoon, Dad asked Steve to meet him in the office, which the two of them were recently sharing. The office was small and had only one desk, with two old armchairs on each side. Dad believed that all he needed was a simple office with very basic furniture. He was happy with his old pickup truck and never considered replacing it. "It runs very well, meeting all what the business needs, and if it breaks down every now and then, I have a very good mechanic to fix it at a decent cost," he used to say.

Dad made two cups of coffee and handed one to Steve. He asked Steve to have a seat and then sat in his old armchair.

"How unusual for Dad to take a coffee break during a work day," Steve thought. He could sense that Dad had something serious on his mind.

Dad took a sip from his mug, looked at Steve and began: "I would like to talk to you son about some important things that I feel I must share with you today. I've been watching your growing involvement in our business and all the hours you have been putting into work. All your life you have had a great sense of decency and honesty, and I know you will keep it. That's how I saw myself years ago when I started out.

"When you returned from college, I wasn't sure you would want to stay with me here. I thought that, like many young men, you would want to pursue your own career. There are so many business graduates who want to work in financial institutions, hoping to make a quick break into the fast money lane and stay there as long as they can. But you didn't choose that road, and I really feel your heart is here. I know you are very ambitious and have some great ideas of how to help our company grow. So I decided to share with you a few things that I learned over the years, which you may not find in any textbook—at least as far as I know."

Dad put down his mug, and Steve was ready for a long speech.

"The first and most vital thing is modesty," Dad continued. "It is a scarce commodity nowadays.

"It should be your main value in life. No matter how financially well-off you will ever be, modesty is what you must retain. It will keep you decent at all times and will never allow success to blind you. It will protect you against ill advice from pseudo friends who like you for your money rather than the real you. It will give you the necessary power to withstand tough times in business and your personal life. And trust me son, crisis always arrive at the least expected times. Therefore, regardless how successful you become, never let it go to your head. Always keep modesty as a key value."

Steve blew at the steam rising from his cup and took another sip as he absorbed Dad's words.

"With that in mind," Dad continued, "there are also other key lessons I would like to share with you, Steve. Many people can learn how to service tools. Over time some of them may even become craftsmen as we are—at least this is my belief of how we are regarded by our customers. You must have enough knowledge, passion and expertise in what you do. It is the first step one has to take when establishing a business in order to become successful. Even if you are a great sales-person, it wouldn't take long for your customers to become disappointed, unless your work is truly high quality."

Dad then stood up. "Let me clarify what I just said." He walked to the old bookcase that was situated at the far end of the office and took out his battered dictionary. He began looking through it and then read aloud the definition of craftsmanship, 'Impressive quality of something made with skill.'

"Steve, that precisely sums up who we are," Dad said passionately. "Nevertheless, there are other things beyond craftsmanship that I would like to share with you. I believe if you truly internalize them, it will allow you to be better than anyone, no matter what you do."

Dad paused and added, "Maybe one day you will be challenged with a different enterprise. One never knows what lies ahead."

Dad sat in his chair, looked at Steve and waited for his son to take all the new information in. He noticed a coffee stain on the desk, rubbed it out with his handkerchief, and then continued. "Before we start discussing the things beyond craftsmanship, I would like to share with you a decision I have made. I wish to retire soon."

He took a deep breath. "All of my life I have worked very hard and spent long hours at work. Now it's time to slow down and spend more quality time with Mom. You know we're not getting younger, and I also need to take care of my health—and there are a lot of things Mom and I would like to do together. I'm sure we'll be busy, especially when we become grand-parents?" Dad added with a smile.

"I've been talking with Mom, and we both agree that it is time to turn over the business to you. I would like to retire within a month or so."

Dad paused for a minute, looking at Steve, trying to gauge his reaction and then said, "There is one more thing you should know, Steve. With the stressful situation of slow down in the economy during the past couple of years, I had to take a few loans from the bank to keep us afloat. With banks feeling the financial crunch as well, they pass it along to their customers—including us. We have to quickly find a way to pay off an outstanding loan and reduce our debts," Dad sighed. "However, our business is picking up and we see positive results on the bottom line."

Dad got up, and with a warm smile shook Steve's hand. "Congratulation son, I'm sure the upward trend will continue, and with your leadership I'm confident we will enjoy a complete turnaround."

While holding Steve's hand he said, "Of course my retirement will not happen until we will resolve the situation with the bank. After that, I will be around and do my best to make myself available for any help or consultation you may need.

"Now let's take a fifteen-minute break. There are some urgent things I have to sort out at the shop, and I'm sure you can use a break too." And then he left the room.

It's More Than Just Craftsmanship

Steve had a long fifteen minutes to think about what he had just heard. "Dad's announcement of his retirement seems way too early. What about his insistence that I learn all aspects of the business from the bottom up before I can assume full responsibility. What is this issue with the bank? It all sounds confusing."

And then a nagging thought crossed his mind. "I wonder what prompted Dad to make such an unexpected move? What could be wrong with him? Is that why he was talking first about values and what is really important in life?"

Steve quickly pushed these thoughts aside. He always had full confidence in Dad. He got off his chair and started walking back and forth in the tiny office.

There was a lot to think about, but he knew that the dynamics of everything had suddenly changed. Immediately he felt the pressure of time. The clock was ticking....

As he was pacing, he thought, "A month, or maybe a little bit more is not a whole lot of time, and the pressure from the bank complicates things even further. Although Dad will still be here after he retires, his availability will gradually diminish. Do I have enough time to acquire sufficient knowledge about fixing tools, let alone other aspects of our business? I'll probably need to get his advice with some complex tool jobs and other pressing issues. But with him retiring so soon, I'm not sure how much time will he be able to give me when I really am in need. I can't believe the business will be resting on my shoulders. I have so little time to get it all together, and it will require intense days and nights."

As he was absorbing the upcoming challenges of a new reality, Steve sat down, grabbed a pencil and wrote on a sheet of paper:

Dad retires within a month

Lessons to be learned:
- Key value in life is "modesty"
- The basics are high "quality" and "capabilities" to establish business

Things beyond craftsmanship ???

Steve's thoughts were interrupted as he heard the office door open. Dad walked in and sat on his chair. Seeing Steve's expression, he decided that getting on with his ideas would be the best way to let Steve digest the news.

"I will share with you later the financial information and our options with the bank—we still have a few cards up our sleeves," Dad said. "So, let's continue from where we left off. Here are the other things beyond craftsmanship and quality that I believe you have to learn—if you want to be better than anyone in our trade. I don't think you will find it in any textbook. In fact, I believe these things are critical to any type of business no matter what you do; it is really what lies behind...."

"Behind what?" Steve interrupted.

"I'm getting there," Dad replied somewhat impatiently. He was far too deep in his explanation.

"When you get a request for fixing a tool, the first thing you really need to do is quickly evaluate what type of service it needs," he said. "Not all tools are serviced in the same way, even for those that look similar. Each tool has its own specific characteristics, requiring attention to the very fine details, almost as if every tool has a life of its own. Even if you have two identical orders, they're still two different types of service, if you look beyond their technical aspects."

"How is it possible that identical orders turn into different types of service?" Steve asked.

"Because you're dealing with different customers," Dad said, pausing. "You must develop the ability to see the customer behind each and every one of the tools we service."

Steve was ready to make a comment but Dad didn't let him cut in.

"If you can do this, the customer will feel it and appreciate you, not just as an exceptional service provider but as a friend," Dad continued. "I emphasize this because it is not something that's a given in every individual. It is something you have to develop until it becomes a natural part within you. Once you do, it will make you different to the others."

There was a moment of silence. Steve got off his chair and began pacing back and forth in the small office, trying to absorb the information.

He finally sat down and said, "So craftsmanship is a key to success and...."

Before Steve could finish, Dad said, "It can get you far, but if you really want to get further you have to take the next step, which is much less tangible. You have to develop the ability to see the customer behind every order and modify your service to fit his or her special needs."

For a moment Dad's explanation sounded too ambiguous, and Steve was ready to interject. But he did not. His respect for Dad and the pure simplicity of the concept allowed Dad to carry on. Steve's self-restraint was about to quickly pay off.

Indirect Sight

While speaking about his concept Dad grabbed a sample tool from the shelf next to his chair. It was one of a few he kept at the office as models. Dad used to show them from time to time when a new customer arrived.

He put the tool on the center of the table and said, "When I look back at the time I started the business, I focused my efforts on proving to potential customers that what we offer is as good as the very best in our line of business. Then I convinced them to try us out. I offered free trials, substantial discounts, and whatnot, just to prove our abilities in competing with the best guys around.

"It was an uphill battle and a constant struggle of balancing between doing what is right, while keeping our efforts within our financial limitations. Our excellence in providing a best quality tool eventually paid off, and we drew in more and more customers.

"But, Steve, after establishing a business of the highest quality, it took me a while to realize that it was not enough to simply be a good craftsman. Over the years I thought a lot about how to improve the way we ran our business.

I looked at our service and tried to compare it to others both inside and outside of our service field. Sometimes when you look outside, you can get some good ideas and implement them successfully into your own situation. I looked at many cases, and it seems as if there are two very different worlds when it comes to service. The first one is the direct service world."

"What does that mean?" Steve asked.

"Well, look at banks, retail stores, beauty salons, restaurants, and even in some public services. Think of what you get there," Dad explained. "You come in, get your service, and leave. The service is provided while you are physically present. So you receive the service directly.

"The other kind is entirely different. It is the indirect service world. Think of what happens with the electricians, plumbers, painters, mechanics, parts manufacturers, and others. There, you are not physically present throughout most of the service."

Steve was surprised by Dad's idea of two different worlds.

"So I presume we belong to the indirect one?" he asked.

"Yes, Steve, we do," Dad answered. "Our customers give us their tools, and we fix them while they are gone."

He pointed at the sample tool. "I'm convinced our world is more complex. In the direct service world, the service provider interacts with the customer while performing the job. In our case we don't. Therefore, in my opinion, our indirect service world is more challenging—at least for those of us who care about our customers.

"Think how simpler the world could be, if people who liked other people would only work in the direct service world," he smiled. "And people who didn't like other people would only provide service indirectly. That way everybody could be happy."

Steve was not an artist. Yet, in his mind he pictured a humorous sketch of Dad's idea. He envisioned happy people directly serving customers while gloomy people would be sitting in dark shops, working behind the scenes, serving their customers from far away.

But even with Dad's amusing scenario in his mind, Steve still saw a conflict. "But, Dad, frequently when I go to a bank I meet gloomy people, yet when I look at people performing indirect services they seem to smile a lot," he said. "It seems that somehow they have switched their roles.

"Well, I'm afraid in reality it is a mixture of both, Steve. And as to people frowning when you go to the bank, maybe they are too busy counting your money," Dad replied laughing.

"Now let's leave jokes behind. In both worlds of direct or indirect service, you have to be professional in what you do. If you are not, it is more likely that you would lose customers and over time lose your livelihood. Doing a good job is the basis for every trade's existence, but it is far from being sufficient unto itself. The interaction with your customer is just as important. And this is where many people fail."

Steve was ready to add a note to his list, but he didn't want to interrupt Dad's explanation.

"In the direct service world, you have a better opportunity to develop these skills," Dad continued. "But even out there it is not obvious to every service provider. However in our case son, it is much more difficult to do since we don't have the customer in front of us whenever we perform a service. We are unable to see how satisfied he or she is and adjust accordingly."

He then said, "If you learn this one notion, Steve, and find the way into your customers' hearts, even when they are not present when you do the job, it will be a springboard for your success. It will turn your service into a very special venture, one that people will want to come back to time after time because not only are they getting an excellent service...they are getting you."

Dad stopped for a moment and looked at his watch. "It is getting late. Mom and I have an important early evening social meeting. We need to expedite our discussion."

A Common Complexity

Dad stood up, stretched a little and walked toward the small cabinet at the corner of the office, hoping to find something to munch on. There was nothing left, so he decided to make more coffee. The short break allowed Steve to gather his thoughts.

"I like Dad's notion and like the springboard for success metaphor, but achieving it may not be that simple. It is complex enough learning the technical details of our trade, and Dad has complicated it even more with his idea of seeing the customer behind every order."

He looked at his paper with his list and realized he did not capture all of Dad's explanation, and added:

Things beyond craftsmanship:

A. Ability to see the customer
   for each service you provide

B. In the "direct" and "indirect"
   service worlds

Dad was back with the fresh pot of coffee. Steve decided to skip coffee and drink some water instead. His face expressed growing concern.

"It all sounds very logical, Dad, but how do you really do it in the indirect service world—to put it more precisely, how do you make it happen in our situation?" he asked politely.

Dad paused. "Our indirect service world is not just about fixing tools. As I said, you must expand the view. For every tool we get, you have to look as though it is the customer himself." He then added. "And you have to do it while you do the repair job—and even when you are not working on it as well."

Steve was baffled. "I get the idea of seeing the customer while working on his order, but what do you mean by visualizing him when not working on it?" he asked.

"You have to look at the queue. A tool awaiting service is no different than a customer waiting in line," Dad answered. "And the longer the line, the more impatient he becomes.

"If we look at what happens in our trade and compare it to someone else's, preferably different to our type of service, we may be able to gain a better understanding. And I think the best is to take the customer's view instead of the service provider."

"What do you have in mind?" Steve asked.

"Let me give you an example from the direct service world," Dad replied. "Think about a hairdresser and her clientele. I'm sure that you as everybody else have had the experience of being served at the barbershop or at the hair salon. I still get my hair cut at my barber, but I notice that these days, unisex salons are taking over. So Steve, do you get your hair cut as soon as you walk in, or do you wait for a while?"

"More often than not I have to wait," Steve answered.

"How long do you usually wait?" Dad asked.

"It varies. Sometimes it is only for a few minutes and other times it's much longer. I guess it depends on how long the line is."

"You see Steve, a tool waiting to be serviced is very similar to you waiting in line for the hairdresser, and as I said the longer the line, the more impatient the customer becomes. Is it really different when it comes to our customers?"

Satisfied with his explanation, Dad carried on. "You have to look at the big picture. The waiting time of the customer and the customer's point of view is what really matters. And it is not just the waiting before service, Steve. It is about what happens within."

"Within what?" Steve asked.

"Within the entire cycle," Dad answered. "Put yourself in the shoes of the customer, Steve. Look at the hair salon example. How long do you have to wait? What happens while you are waiting until you leave? How does the hairdresser welcome you? Are you greeted with a smile? Does she pay any attention to you while you wait? Are you offered a cup of coffee—and is there any small talk? And when you finally get to the chair are you treated as royalty?

Dad took a breath. "With all that, let's not forget about quality. The hairdresser still has to perform the service you ask, and this is where her craftsmanship and professional skills come to play. But even after the haircut, the hairdresser's job is not over yet. As she finishes her tasks, hopefully to your fullest satisfaction, the way she interacts with you until you leave her hair salon is also a part of her service. So you see, Steve, it is not just a hairstyling job. A common visit to the hairdresser is in fact a multi-step process, and every element of it is critical. It is about the whole service cycle and the attention the customer receives throughout."

Dad paused, giving Steve time to digest the concept and then summarized:

"So it's more than just craftsmanship. If the hairdresser is able to give you the highest quality service and make you feel special throughout your entire stay, I guarantee that you will come back. It is not a one-time shot. It is essential for her to sustain it for *every* service she is giving, now and in the future. In return, you are likely to become a loyal customer, who will eventually spread the word around."

Dad looked at his watch. "You have to excuse me for a minute, Steve. I must call Mom now."

"Tell her I said hello," Steve said. "Do you mind if I step outside while you make your call? Some fresh air would really help to clear my mind."

"Sure you can," Dad answered, appreciating Steve's sensitivity.

He picked up the phone as Steve stepped out.

The Hairdresser and Ourselves

5:00 p.m.

"I'm still discussing with Steve some important issues," he told Mom, lowering his voice. "I already conveyed to him what we have discussed with regard to future plans. I need a few more minutes to close things up. How much time do I have so we won't be late for our meeting?"

"We will be fine if you're home within thirty minutes," Mom replied.

"So I will see you soon dear," Dad said, and he hung up the phone.

Steve was back at the office a couple of minutes after Dad had finished his call. He sat down and drank some water. "After having a break and some fresh air, can we talk about how to take these ideas and apply them to our business?"

Dad was ready to answer, but he stopped there. "Wait, Steve, I realized the hairdresser cycle is not complete yet. I missed an important part."

"I thought you covered it all, Dad. Taking the customer view I can't see what is missing."

"What's missing is the process before getting in for the first time," Dad replied.

"Well, I already agreed that I probably had to wait in line a little bit, and it would likely happen again on my next visit," Steve said.

"No no, maybe I'm not making myself clear," Dad said. "Just think about what happened back when you booked your first appointment? When you called, how did the hairdresser welcome you over the phone? Did you receive a warm welcome? Was she able to schedule your upcoming appointment to your satisfaction? That is another part of the cycle. It starts when you book your appointment and it ends when you leave her salon after receiving your haircut.

"I guarantee you that no matter how good she is, if your expectation for service is a maximum of one week and the next opening she has is in four weeks, you are likely go somewhere else—unless she happens to be highly sought after. But as it often happens with famous hairstylists, she may not even care," Dad chuckled. "In such a case, you simply have to wait."

Dad felt he had covered all aspects of her cycle, and now attempted to relate it to their own business. "Look how challenging it is for such an interpersonal service," Dad said. "Not only does the hairdresser have to be excellent in hairstyling, but she has to carry that excellence throughout her whole service process. But you see Steve, our business is different. We provide service indirectly. Yet you have to be special for your customer, in what you make and how you make it, throughout the entire process—even though the customer is not present at the time of service."

Dad stopped for a moment and looked at Steve. "I think that sums it up, and it can serve as a good start. There are a lot of details to be explored in order to make the concept work, and eventually we will get there too."

Dad got up and put his arm on Steve's shoulders. "All I'm able to offer is my experience and time. I have seen a lot, and yet, even I don't fully understand what the right answers are. Sometimes it feels like the more I see, the less I know. However, looking back, I can at least share with you some of my thoughts and understanding."

He then sat back in his chair. "Too often people start their business journey focusing on what they know and love best—the making of their product or service. Unfortunately, many miss the critical aspect: giving enough attention to the entire cycle of interaction with their customers. It isn't obvious to everyone. More often than not, you as a customer, meet people who provide an excellent product, but who lack the basics of interpersonal skills, and boy, that's such a turnoff!

"What makes it even worse, is the fact that they are unaware of their total service cycle. There are so many people who have a great gift in their craftsmanship. Yet, their inability to connect with the customer throughout the entire cycle creates a major roadblock for their business. What's really sad is that they will never realize why their major life investment has never taken off."

Dad paused, "In fact, you don't have to be a business owner or an entrepreneur—these concepts really apply to everybody. Even if you don't sell goods or services, just being at work and interacting with a co-worker, another department, or serving the public, puts you in that position—providing service to other people."

Dad stood up, stretched a little, and walked toward the coat rack on the other side of the room. "So, Steve," he said, swinging his coat on, "what would you do to guarantee that every tool we service will be treated through its entire cycle, the same way a customer would be treated at a successful hair salon? I apologize for not being able to continue our discussion as I'm already late, and Mom is waiting for me to take her to an important social meeting. I suggest we carry on our conversation tomorrow," Dad said as he headed out, leaving Steve behind to think.

Changing Seats

Steve stood beside the window, gazing at the cloudy skies just as it began to get dark outside. He knew that unlike his dad, he was not going to be free for any social events for a long time. Adjusting the old armchair, he tried to put things in order. He ran all the many conversations he'd had with his father through his head: everything he knew or thought he knew about the business, what he had learned in school, and especially what he had heard from Dad earlier that evening.

"Key values, craftsmanship and beyond, tools to be treated as customers, service cycles and what not; and Dad turning over his lifetime kingdom to me. So within a couple of months I will be on my own, and on top of everything: the bank's financial pressure must be resolved."

Steve was not able to get his new impression of Dad out of his mind. He never expected to hear such things from his father. He had a great respect and love for him, but in his mind Dad was a pragmatic person, always placing high demands on himself as well as on others—a great craftsman and someone who was the best in his trade. Sometimes he was too tough, a perfectionist for traditional values. He knew that Dad had built the business from scratch, and his qualities were probably the key ingredients for its success.

But today he had learned something new about his father. He expected to learn how to fix tools, but instead, he was learning how tools could become the reflection of their owner, the customer—and about their service cycles. He had never guessed that Dad had such a high sensitivity for the finer aspects of treating his customers.

These were things that Steve had not learned in school. He had studied math, complicated business models, quantitative methods, and optimization functions to maximize profits. However, what he had learned today from Dad's simple wisdom and sensitivity was entirely something else. Steve couldn't believe how much his father had opened up to him in such a short span of time.

He got up and walked to the other side of the room to fill his glass with fresh water. He went back and looked at his notes on the other side of the table. While standing, he read carefully through his key points.

He then sat in his chair and tried to put things in a logical order. "We have our customers, and they trust us to service their tools with the highest quality. If I look close enough, I may be able to find each customer's unique imprint in every tool we service. As Dad said, two identical tools requiring the same service are really two different entities if they come from two different customers."

Then it crossed his mind, "It is not different from two customers coming to the hairdresser during the day, one in the morning and one in the afternoon. Imagine both are blondes with the same hair length, who happen to want a short haircut. They point at the same model in a beauty magazine and wish to emulate her hairstyle. From the dry aspects of service, it should take the same amount of time and effort for the hairdresser to do their hair. Yet, each one would like to receive attention based on her individual personality. At the end of the day they both will be happy, as long as they will not bump into each other at the same party!

"So how do I bridge these ideas to our reality? At the hairdressing salon, as challenging as it may be, it is still simpler to do since the hairdresser interacts directly with her customer at the time of service. How can we do it in our shop, where we don't provide direct service to our customers? Maybe Dad found a way to do it, and over the years it became part of him. But how do I take this intuitive knowledge and make it a part of me, without struggling for years?"

The thought of Dad and seeing his empty seat provoked Steve's mind. "Maybe I should change seats. Sometimes it can give a better perspective," and with this thought he got up, took his notes list and sat in Dad's chair. Because of his high regard for his father, Steve was always careful not to sit in Dad's armchair. But the special circumstances made him break his rule. After all, he was soon to take the lead. He re-read his notes and it was as if they projected a deeper meaning.

Maybe sitting in Dad's chair gave Steve a new view, or perhaps simply the act of changing seats.

"It's really all in understanding the DNA!" he said excitedly.

The idea of the two identical tools at their shop and the two blondes at the hair salon, suddenly clicked.

"A successful hairdresser would intuitively modify her service for each customer according to their individual personality and unique aspects; and so should we!" Steve concluded.

"We must find a methodical way to do the same as what she naturally does. It is really putting the customers' DNA in front of us while providing service. That is what the hairdresser does and probably what Dad has developed over the years for each of our customers."

Excited about his new *customer's DNA* discovery, Steve got off Dad's chair, took a few steps away and things became even clearer. "It is customer DNA which, if you know how to use it correctly, will give you the best results," he thought. "The combination of craftsmanship and customer DNA know-how will give you the edge. I think I'm finally getting it!"

Changing seats can transform one's perspective, and Steve did not yet know how much role playing lay ahead of him.

A Short Interruption

The old phone, which was placed on the table near Dad's armchair, rang. Steve, who was a short distance away, quickly picked up the phone. "Hello, how can I help you?" he said. There was the noise of a bad line connection and Steve couldn't hear anything clearly. He said hello again, and this time the line quality was slightly better. He could faintly hear a voice on the other side—only picking a few broken words. "I can't hear you well, can you speak louder?" he asked. And the voice was fading. "Well I am sorry but I can't hear anything, can you call again?" Steve asked, and was ready to hang up the phone.

Suddenly the line connection was clear and he could hear, "Hello, hello, can you hear me now? I am Bupti from the...." The voice faded again and then it peaked, "I am calling regarding...." and the call was disconnected.

Steve waited for a minute or two. The phone did not ring again. "The line connection sounded as if the call was made from far away," he thought.

From the few words he heard, he had detected a foreign accent, but he wasn't sure of its origin. "Probably someone dialed a wrong number," he concluded.

"I can check the phone number by looking at the caller ID," he thought, but couldn't. Dad's phone was too old—the kind that didn't have an incoming call indicator.

Customer DNA

The short interruption helped Steve to refocus his thoughts. He sat back in his chair, took a sip of water, and looked at his notes. He felt very proud of his new discovery. "It is the first step of getting science into the grinding practicality of life. Customer DNA is a key to breaking new ground," he thought.

"Maybe I should summarize Dad's experience and my customer DNA idea in a few bullet points," he thought. "It'll help me internalize how everything should work."

He grabbed another piece of paper and wrote:

If I will be able to adjust my service to my customer DNA,

I will be able to push limits and grow

Steve looked carefully at his summary sentence and felt something was missing, but couldn't figure out what it was. He tried over and over to find the missing part, but felt like he was caught in a loop. Frustrated, he got up and stretched as he looked through the window. It was already dark outside.

With all the excitement and intense events, Steve realized he did not have a chance to share the news with his girlfriend. He picked up the phone and called her.

"Hello darling, I really miss you," she greeted him happily. "You probably had another long tough day."

"Yes I have," Steve sighed, "but it was a most unusual one." And he shared with Sharon Dad's unexpected decision, along with the sudden burden of having to learn everything—and become the leader of the company almost immediately. He then briefed her on everything that had transpired since late afternoon. However, he decided not to bring up the financial situation with the bank, and his concern of Dad's reasons for his announcement.

Needless to say Sharon was taken by surprise at hearing the news, but quickly offered Steve the bright side of his new responsibility. "Your decision to stick with Dad seems to have paid off sooner than expected. You know I will stand by you all along the way."

"I probably need all the help I can get," he replied. "I really appreciate your support. I'm sure it will help me put things in better perspective and get the most out of the new circumstances."

Steve shared with her some of Dad's life experience and the lessons he offered. He told her of craftsmanship and beyond, and about the hairdresser example. But above all, he told her proudly about his idea of the customer's DNA and then said, "Sharon, do you mind if I read you my summary sentence?" And so he did.

She was silent for a moment and then said, "It is a nice way to put it, but I think there are a couple of issues to consider. How do you implement the DNA idea, and how do you make sure your customer is fully satisfied along the entire process?"

Steve was quick to respond, "Well I think that..." and then he paused mid thought. "Sharon, those are two very good questions, and behind them lie some interesting suggestions. I guess I have a lot of work ahead of me. I'll probably be staying at the office for a little longer."

They talked for a while and ended the conversation by blowing each other a kiss over the phone.

Steve went back to the grind. He decided to re-examine everything that Dad had told him, and there was plenty to think about. Dad's words about how each tool has a life of its own—not just in the making but also by what is reflected from its customer—echoed in his mind.

It triggered a thought of past meetings with Dad, himself, and some of their employees, discussing problems of salvaging badly damaged tools—and finding bright solutions to bring the tools back to life. It had always brought the highest level of satisfaction and pride. But with his new understanding, it gave Steve an entirely different view.

"It's like falling in the trap of the technical aspects, which too many people have a tendency to do," he thought. "It really means concentrating only on the tangible aspect of the service. But what about the intangible side? What about the customer throughout the whole cycle? Did we give any thought to it during our meetings? I can't even imagine what would happen if the hairdresser focused on the hair-styling as her only job, and ignored the customer for the rest of the time."

He looked at his paper and added to his sentence the customer's cycle aspect:

> If I will be able to adjust my service to my customer DNA,
>
> > from initial contact to delivery <
>
> I will be able to push limits and grow

He had changed the concept to include the broad aspect of the whole service—from the beginning to the end.

Steve was proud that he had managed to capture the essence of Dad's experience in one short sentence. He felt it was a good time to wrap things up, but Sharon's questions were still unsettled in his mind.

"How do I implement the DNA idea?" He wondered. "Using something which seems so vague, how do we make sure that our customer is fully satisfied along the entire process? If I ask the hairdresser or anybody else, 'what is customer's DNA?' will I get a clear answer?"

There were too many unanswered questions. Yet, Steve felt ready to call off the long day, go home, and get some rest. "I will try to get more answers tomorrow. I better call Sharon and tell her I'm on my way."

He then began collecting his personal items. They were spread all over the table, as if they were a reflection of the storm of thoughts that had been running through his head during the past few hours. But the storm was far from being over. The thought of Sharon and her unsettling questions had triggered what was to become a very long night.

Sharon and Amos

7:00 p.m.

Steve's mind was going faster than a Japanese bullet train. Looking at his note about customer DNA, he began thinking about his personal experience as a customer—and how he was treated from the moment he had a need for something, all the way until receiving it. The more he thought about it, the more their recent home renovation project, and the experience Sharon had had with Amos, came to mind.

Sharon had been Steve's high school sweetheart. All through college, they never missed an opportunity to be together. Steve had studied business and Sharon had studied English and the Arts. Although studying at different colleges, they had always spent time with each other during holidays and school breaks.

After they graduated from college, and with Steve's decision to continue working with Dad, Sharon had found a teaching job in their town. They had decided to live together before tying the knot. But as a young couple at the beginning of their careers, they could only afford a small house.

Not long after moving in, they decided to renovate the house. Each brought in some used furniture from their parents' homes, and had worked weekends to put everything in order. They did everything they could by themselves: yard work, painting, replacing carpet, modifying the old kitchen and organizing cabinets—all to shape it into a nice cozy home.

From time to time they had to use some help from professionals like carpenters and plumbers, if they didn't have the knowledge or the time. As beginners with a relatively low income, all of the remodeling and repair work was done under a tight budget. They did everything they could to cut costs while shopping around. With Steve's focus on craftsmanship and Sharon's upbringing in the arts, they wouldn't compromise on esthetics and quality. Whenever they encountered a budget problem, they preferred to delay purchasing rather than settling for lower quality.

However, the one exception was Sharon's grandmother's old sofa, which had been in Sharon's family for generations. Made of cherry wood, it was a unique piece of furniture, handcrafted by an unknown carpenter. But its age showed. The upholstery was in bad condition, the fabric color had faded a long time ago, and it was badly stained. In some parts the fabric was torn, the cushions were worn out, and the wood was covered with scratches. Many people would think, "Why keep it?" and simply would have put it on the curb. However, for this kind of sofa even nowadays, you would not just leave it out on the street or put it in a garage sale. In a small Midwest town where basic values are still ingrained in peoples' nature, even a much less exclusive piece of furniture gets a second life before being trashed. But you don't have to live in small town America to appreciate the value of things you have purchased a long time ago. Especially when the economy is tight, you would think twice before throwing them out.

For Sharon, her grandma's old sofa was something special. It had senti-mental value with her family history, made with a craftsmanship scarcely found nowadays. In her artistic mind, she could see how it could be turned into a unique feature in the center of the living room. She did not live in one of those big cities where people spend a lot of money collecting antique furniture. She had a limited budget, yet had the artistic gift to make the sofa fit into any upscale New York City apartment.

Although he was unable to visualize Sharon's plans for the old couch, Steve went along with her vision. In her mind she could see every detail of the sofa, including the new fabric color and pattern, the wood finish, and cushions. She could also picture where exactly it would be situated in the living room. He agreed to put it top of the budget list. After all, she was the artist and he was the businessman.

Sharon contacted Amos, the best upholsterer in the entire county, to come as soon as possible to see the old sofa and give her a quote for the work. His shop was in another small town located about forty miles away, but for his reputation it was worth the extra cost of shipping back and forth. Not only was Amos known to be very creative and thorough in his work, but he was a very courteous and friendly person. Steve had got his name through Dad, as Amos had been running his business almost as long as Dad had. Not only that, but Mom used Amos's services to remake a few items of furniture in their house over the years. Steve did not know about this until he had asked Dad if he knew of someone who could help in repairing furniture. Funny how much you can learn when things become important and they really matter to you.

A few days later, Amos came to Steve and Sharon's house. His old pickup truck was parked outside. The house renovation work was getting close to completion. Amos took a look at the sofa, and Sharon tried to explain how and what should be done. With great passion she told him about the sofa's history and its importance in keeping the family heritage. She did the best she could to express her artistic idea, drawing some sketches and pointing out the details that were important to her.

Amos pulled out his measuring tape, measured the sofa from all angles, and asked Sharon if he could have a copy of her sketches. She ran downstairs, and within a few minutes she came back with a couple of copies and handed them to Amos. He wrote the measurements on the sketches and after making some calculations, he gave an estimated price, noting it could vary depending on type of fabric. They also discussed the type of wood finish that would remove the scratches. Amos estimated that the job could be completed in about four weeks after choosing the fabric and finalizing the order—a week to receive the fabric and three more weeks to finish the job.

The sofa's promised delivery time coincided perfectly with Sharon's schedule. Family and friends were invited to celebrate the house renovation completion. She was trying to align all the open jobs to be completed a week prior to the planned party date. The upcoming event was very important for Sharon, and she told Amos how she envisioned the sofa being a centerpiece in the living room.

Sharon didn't want to lose any time. The next day she was at Amos's shop, looking at several fabric catalogs and wood finish samples. Not only did Amos deal with fabrics, padding, and cushions, but over the years he added wood finishing to his services, giving him an edge over the competition. He charged more than most of his competitors. But the quality and reliability of his services, along with the wood finishing kept his shop busy, sometimes very busy.

Within a couple of hours, Sharon had selected the desired fabric and the wood finish, and Amos then finalized the order. She had chosen a special greenish-gray fabric that would give the sofa an antique look with a modern touch.

The sofa was picked up by Amos's truck the following day. The clock started ticking. It was only four weeks away from the promised delivery date.

Three weeks passed by. Steve and Sharon were both busy trying to complete the last few tasks at the house. Like most projects, things seemed to pile up toward the end, putting a lot of pressure on both of them. The final details and fine-tuning took much more effort than originally planned.

Steve looked at the list of tasks to be finished and the sofa item was still uncrossed, which prompted him to ask Sharon if she'd heard from Amos. She had not.

A few minutes later she was on the phone talking to Amos, wondering if her sofa was going to be ready on time.

"A couple of my guys are working on it right now at full speed," Amos said. "We received the fabric a bit late, and there were some other problems at the shop. The wood finish is almost complete, and it came out really nicely. We will do our best to deliver on time. I will call you the moment it will be ready."

A week passed by. The sofa was supposed to be already delivered, but it was not. The house party was only a week away. For the next few days, a new ritual had developed between Sharon and Amos. Sharon called every day to check on the sofa, and Amos promised to do his best to finish it within a couple of days, and so on it went. The pressure of the upcoming party was high, and although the sofa was already late for its promised date, Sharon was still hoping to get the sofa on the morning of the open house event, just before guests would show up.

In the end, the sofa did not arrive, but Sharon could not delay the party. Everybody was complimenting the couple on how beautiful the house was and what a great job they had done. But the masterpiece—the sofa that was supposed to be in the center of the living room—was missing. Sharon was incredibly disappointed.

Finally, it was ready after six and a half weeks, two and a half weeks later than promised. When Amos called Sharon to schedule a delivery, she could feel how uneasy he was with the entire situation. She sensed he was under lot of pressure. At first, she associated it with the way he felt about being late, which was partially true.

However, to Sharon's dismay, instead of just apologizing for his lateness, Amos kept talking about his entire shop being overcrowded with a lot of unfinished furniture. He complained about how he was forced to use his "ready to be delivered" storage space for holding work in progress. It was all so busy, Amos said, that if he did not deliver some finished items, including Sharon's sofa, he would have to keep them in an open area outside. That certainly was not good for the furniture. He also mentioned how he had an influx of new orders in recent weeks, causing him to juggle work priorities and have late deliveries.

Amos is a nice guy, and Sharon is a fine lady with great manners and a lot of patience. However, she felt she had to use all of her self-restraint to keep from erupting.

"Instead of me telling him how I feel, he is telling me his problems," she told Steve later. But Sharon's nature and her good upbringing, held her back from telling Amos what was really on her mind. One can only imagine what would have happened had Amos worked in New York City and faced an upset customer after such a delay.

When the sofa was eventually delivered, it was beautiful. The wood finish was as promised and so was the quality of the work, but what of the fabric color? It wasn't exactly what Sharon had ordered; at least not the way she remembered seeing it in the catalog six and half weeks earlier at Amos's shop. Maybe it was her memory, or perhaps it was the different lighting in his shop than in her house?

She couldn't restrain herself from expressing her frustration. Amos suggested coming by with the catalog and comparing it to the sofa fabric. There was a distinct difference between the colors. Sharon's memory and artistic skills were right. Amos said that often there could be variations in colors between the catalog and the actual fabric and not just in Sharon's case.

"A production batch at the fabric factory could be different to the one in the catalog, hence the slight variation," he explained. Then adding salt to Sharon's open wound, when she sat on the sofa it was not as comfortable as she expected. The sofa cushions were hard and felt too firm. When she brought it up to Amos, he suggested that over time they would get softer, noting that there were three levels of firmness: hard, medium, and soft. Based on his experience, he had used the hard grade for better durability and value. Sharon was unaware of these options and probably would have chosen the medium grade for more comfort.

After seeing all the different problems of the order—the delivery delay, color difference, cushion firmness and Sharon's overall dissatisfaction—Amos offered to change the fabric and the cushions to whatever she wanted, at no additional cost. For Amos it was not a common gesture and would cause him to lose a great deal of money on this job. Being sensitive to Sharon's acute dissatisfaction and his longtime relationship with Steve's family, Amos was ready to take the loss. But Sharon did not choose another color. She didn't want to be without her sofa for another six weeks, or even longer. After a while she got used to it, even with the different fabric color. It was a beautiful piece after all—one that could nicely decorate any upscale apartment in New York City.

Duality and Miserable Performance Race

Still sitting in the office that night, it was all fresh in Steve's mind. The sofa story seemed to have a happy ending, but it did not. The house party had not been long ago, and the impression of the sofa renovation events continued to trouble Steve. "In the end, Sharon had to compromise and I was left puzzled," he thought.

"What went wrong with Amos that made him so late?" Steve wondered. "Why was the restored sofa different from what Sharon expected in its fabric color and cushion softness? In the beginning everything seemed to work very well, but something went totally wrong in the end."

He couldn't come to any conclusion. He looked around until his eyes locked on Dad's empty armchair. A thought then crossed his mind. "Changing seats, as I did earlier, can give you a different view. Maybe Amos, being our service provider, saw things entirely different from Sharon and I—his customers."

Steve carried the thought further, "Dad had started talking about our business and it wasn't long before he suggested taking the customer perspective. That's how we got into discussing the hair salon. Sharon's sofa experience was based on her view as a customer. Did Amos try to change his perspective, taking a different angle? Is it possible that what we saw as a failure looked to him as providing a good service?"

Amos was not there to answer Steve's question. The only thing he could do was to put himself in Amos's shoes. Instantly Steve found himself supporting Amos's case. After all, he could identify with him as being a service provider. In a split second he felt like a totally different person. His professional pride immediately kicked in. He attempted to rationalize the situation, but he stopped before getting carried away.

It took him a minute to digest the situation "What had really happened to me? How come without hesitation I switched from being along with Sharon, to taking Amos's side?"

Steve got up, walked to the small kitchenette next to the office and splashed his face with cold water. It helped him to get a clearer view—of the customer and the service giver. "Perhaps it all stems from the role we take—the disturbing duality we have as being customers versus being service providers. How come what we demand as customers, too often we fail to provide—once we switch roles to become service givers?"

The thought was too troubling to ignore. He returned to his seat, and then it occurred to him that he is not alone.

"It doesn't really matter what you do," Steve concluded. "Whenever you are at work, you are a service provider. Even if you don't sell goods or services, just being at work and interacting with a co-worker puts you in that position. Then, when you look to buy something, you become a customer. So in essence everybody acts in two roles—being a service provider and a customer. And it can even happen within the same day!"

Steve didn't have a clear answer for the duality problem. But he felt, that as a service provider, the answer lies in perusing the way Dad had suggested—changing to the seat of the customer view.

He decided to re-examine their house renovation project. "What made us satisfied with all the service givers, except Amos? Was it their professional credibility, did they have less time pressure, or was it something else?"

He examined other possibilities, but couldn't come to any significant conclusion. "The carpenter, the plumber, the electrician, and a few others who worked in the house renovation project, were all under a tight schedule to meet the finishing line before the upcoming party. Each had had some problems along the way, but the one that stood above all was Amos the upholsterer."

Then it dawned on him. "It's in the house! That is what put Amos apart from the others. They all did the work in the house. Sharon and I had a daily interaction with each one of them with the exception of Amos. He did his work in his shop forty miles away, and we did not have a clue what was going on.

"It is as though our close interaction transformed the carpenter, the plumber and the electrician to 'an almost-direct service' providers. It probably allowed them to better read our personalities and special requirements. We were able to communicate exactly what we wanted. But it was not the case with Amos.

"With him, we only communicated in the very beginning and at the end. It started very well when Amos came to the house and when Sharon visited his shop the day after. Communication started again right before delivery and at the time of delivering the sofa. But in between there was a big void. There was practically no communication or ongoing interaction. That's what probably sets him apart from the others."

He took a long breath. "I wonder what would have happened if we had communicated with the carpenter, the electrician, and the plumber only once a week rather than every day. I bet they would be late and wouldn't have met our exact expectations as well. And if we were to do it only once every other week or even once a month, I'm sure they would also be standing with Amos on the *miserable performance pedestal*."

In his mind Steve could picture Amos and the other professionals who worked in their house, all competing who would win the 'miserable performance' track and field race—if they were all given equal terms. It didn't take him long to depict it in a sketch.

But in reality Amos was standing there all alone.

Amos's Dichotomy

Steve was pleased with his field-and-track sketch and the concept behind it. "I better run this by Sharon when I get home." He looked at his watch and realized that it probably would not happen that night. By the time he got home, it would be too late for a discussion.

His papers and sketches were spread all over the table. While organizing them, his eyes caught his DNA note. "So adjusting service to customer's DNA, from initial contact to delivery, is the key. It really boils down to the way the service provider and the customer interact along the service cycle. It is up to the provider to make sure he or she understands best what the customer really wants and his unique aspects—the essence of customer DNA.

"And it is wrong to expect the customer to be the pusher and the watchdog for the service supplier."

Steve ran through his experiences as a customer. "As a customer I expect service to be given as soon as possible with good quality and a reasonable price. But what about the service providers, do we always meet our customer expectations?

He expanded his thoughts to other places alike and imagined how he had been treated during service. Dry cleaning stores, auto repair shops, department stores, banks, restaurants, government services, healthcare, and a host of other service providers came to mind; and the list was very long. "Do they think of their job as only one sided? Or do they think of the service they give with the same eyes as those of their customers?"

"I can use this logic to check what might have gone wrong with Amos. It will allow me to better define his performance in meeting Sharon's expectations. From there, I can probably learn the right things to do in our business."

He began to examine Amos's service cycle of the sofa from the first time Sharon contacted him, all the way to delivery.

"Did Amos understand Sharon's customer DNA? Maybe being a craftsman, he might have been too focused on the technical details of renovating the sofa. Quality of work is part of Amos's reputation. It is what we expected and I don't see a problem there. However, he must have missed Sharon's artistic abilities and her attention to detail. She had handed him her sketches and pointed out the details of what she expected. But he did not capture her special requirements for the sofa restoration. Besides writing some measurements, Amos did not take notes at the time of visit, and I doubt if he did later. He must have misread her personality and unique aspects as a customer."

Steve then looked at another important aspect. "Sharon was talking about the open house party and its planned date. She was very excited about it and mentioned how having the sofa in the center of the living room was very important to her. Did Amos miss that? I did not see him making any note such as, *must not miss delivery date*.

And the gap between Sharon and Amos seemed even wider.

"Overall, I think Amos was focused on the sofa renovation and overlooked Sharon as the person behind the order," Steve concluded. "And with the passage of time, coupled with the excessive workload he had, Sharon's sofa was just another job in Amos's shop—one of very many."

He was happy with his assessment, yet his intuition was telling him that it was incomplete.

"Maybe by being personally involved I put emotions ahead of logic," he thought. He was looking for a better way to objectively assess the gap between the two sides—the customer and the provider. Eventually his analytical nature led him to finding the solution.

"For a more precise evaluation, I'll use a school grading method where A is very good and F is failure," he thought and began analyzing Amos's performance:

"The only thing I would give Amos a grade A is for his work quality. For meeting customer specification, I would probably give him C. For meeting time requirements, I would give Amos grade F—it was a total failure!

"But what about communicating with Sharon along the entire cycle? It was pretty good only at the very beginning. Then it was close to nothing. It was even a turnoff when Sharon was calling him and not getting a clear answer. At the time she felt she was getting the runaround. If I look at the entire seven week cycle, from the time Sharon called Amos to the time the sofa was delivered, the grade for attention and making Sharon feeling special wouldn't be more than a D.

"So what is his overall grade? When the work quality is good, but delivery is very late while not meeting specifications, it is almost as though nothing else really matters. So my overall grade for Amos is D, or between D and F."

But before reaching a final verdict Steve switched to take Amos's perspective. "It is amazing how things look different the moment you change your role from being a customer to being the service supplier. As the customer you give Amos an overall grade of a D or even F. But if you put yourself in his shoes as the service provider, you probably would give yourself a totally different grade."

He could imagine Amos defending his case: "I know I was late in delivery. But the delay in getting the fabric from my vendor was part of the reason for being late. It was beyond my control. So I would probably grade myself at B for delivery. From the workmanship aspect, even Sharon was pleased with the quality of work. Here I would grade it as an A.

"For meeting her specifications, I think I did a good job. She was a bit concerned about the fabric color and cushion firmness, but we sorted it out. So in my opinion an A grade would be fair, but I would accept a B."

In his mind Steve could picture Amos becoming even more passionate while presenting his views: "I offered Sharon to replace the fabric and the cushions at no cost just to make her happy, even though it would be a financial loss. So with all fairness my overall grade should at least be between A to B."

Steve felt like he was on stage doing a one-person show and switching from one character to another. One moment he was Sharon and then another moment he'd switch convincingly to become Amos.

He then ran through his mind the other characters he could represent. He was the customer at the hair salon and then could easily switch to being the hairdresser. Similarly he could play the roles of the electrician, the plumber, and the carpenter while working in his house—and also act as their customer. "I could write a whole screenplay and act on behalf of every one of its characters. Hey, maybe I could even act on behalf of Dad, defending his case in front of a customer. Then I could take the customer side. Would it be much different from what Sharon would say to Amos? I bet the gap would be wider than anticipated—not only for us, but for most people as well."

And then he noted with a smile, "I should not forget to play myself as well".

With this imaginary scene he could envision the dichotomy of Amos, alongside many service givers—arguing his A grade on one side of the stage while Sharon, the customer, disputes it and demotes it to an F in front of an applauding audience.

Are We in the Same Trap?

It took Steve a few minutes to shake out Amos's dichotomy stage scene, with the tempting possibility of pursuing screenplay writing and acting as a new career. He looked at his watch and couldn't believe how fast time had flown by. But he felt that having too many unanswered questions would cause him to lose sleep all night.

He was back to the realism of life. "For a service provider like Amos, receiving an overall grade of F or even D from the customer does not make any sense. How is it possible that someone who is so highly regarded in craftsmanship could get such a horrible grade? Is it possible that Dad and I would be in a similar situation like Amos? And what is scarier, is the thought that we might have not been aware of the implications at all."

The more Steve thought about it, the more he was concerned.

"Sharon is only one customer out of many. So maybe it was a onetime fluke and my overall grade does not do justice to Amos. But Amos was telling Sharon how his entire shop was crowded with a lot of unfinished furniture—almost to the point where he was forced to store the finished furniture outside. What does it tell about his service to other customers? Was he late there as well?

"He also mentioned how he got overloaded with new orders, causing him to juggle work priorities and be late with deliveries. Probably Amos and his staff were so overloaded that it caused them to overlook work details and their customers as well. Does Amos have a method to tell him how he is performing with all of his customers? Probably he doesn't; but one thing I'm sure of—we don't have one either."

He was extremely disturbed.

"It's mind boggling. My experience as a customer shows me that this problem exists in many other places, probably more than I ever imagined. Maybe too many people are caught in a similar trap like Amos. Perhaps we are too?"

It's All in Dad's Head

10:00 p.m.

The old phone near Dad's armchair rang. Steve got off his chair, picked up the handset and greeted with a welcoming hello. But there was nobody on the other side. There was a prolonged background noise and then the line was cut off. "It's late at night," Steve thought, as he wondered who might have called.

Instinctively he thought of tracking the incoming call number, but that was impossible. "We should soon replace the phone with a new one that has a caller ID feature," he thought.

The odd time for an office call and the line noise bothered Steve. His mind was back to the bad connection call he received earlier. "Maybe it's the same guy with the foreign accent who called a few hours ago?"

He wasn't sure if it was the late hour that made him suspicious, or was it simply his intuition. But there was nothing he could do to find who might have called.

Steve used the unexpected break to stretch a little, refilled his glass with fresh water and sat in his chair. He gathered his thoughts and continued where he was cut off.

"How do I translate these ideas into actions? It has two sides. One is the customer's DNA. The other is more tangible—about customer specifications, quality, and time requirements.

He started with the first side. "Can I come up with an accurate way to characterize customer DNA? Probably not. Customer DNA sounds vague and is based on intuition. But there must be a way to depict it."

He thought about how Amos, Sharon or Dad would describe customers' DNA, but he felt a successful hairdresser could possibly give the best answer. "Being in the direct service gives her the edge."

With this in mind, Steve carried on. "I wonder what the hairdresser would say about the two blonde ladies asking for the same style? Maybe she would say one is friendly, easygoing, and fairly flexible with a great love of fashion. She'd describe the other one as conservative, formal, quiet—somewhat introverted. I bet she would intuitively process this information in her mind and adjust her service to fit both of them to their fullest satisfaction, even though the work she does is almost the same."

And then he realized, "Maybe one doesn't need to be a psychologist analyzing the patient for hours, writing complex notes and capturing all deep aspects of personality. For most of us it may become very convoluted. Perhaps we just need to use basic intuition and a few simple characteristics to depict a customer personality.

"So it seems that in just a few simple words, using your own language, you can describe a customer. And similar to a successful hairdresser, I believe that each of us is capable of doing it."

The ambiguity of his customer DNA idea suddenly seemed to disappear, and Steve was ready to deal with the other side—the more tangible one.

"Specifications, quality, and time requirements are very important. Without having them in a clear form, it is almost impossible to do a good job—especially when trying to tailor them to the customer DNA.

He was thinking who would be the best to discuss it with. "Sharon does not have the experience, Amos is unavailable and it's impractical to talk to the hairdresser. Dad would probably be the best."

Steve looked at his watch. It was after ten o'clock at night. He could not believe how quickly the time had flown by. "It's a bit late, but maybe I can still call Dad?" So he did. Dad had answered the phone.

"Hi Dad, I'm sorry calling that late, but I have an important subject I hope we can discuss," Steve said. "It wouldn't take long. By the way, did you call a few minutes ago?"

"No, I didn't," Dad answered, surprised that Steve was still at work. "Mom and I just got back home from our social engagement."

Steve excitedly shared with him his latest discovery of customer DNA. It needed some clarifications and when Steve felt he got his message across, he asked Dad for his opinion.

"Think about two customers asking to get our service for two identical tools," Dad replied. "Each one sees his own order, but we see two identical orders that require the same service. If you just look at the dry technical aspects, we have to perform the same job on both. However, if you take a step beyond and ask a few more questions, you may discover that although for you it's the same, for the customers it's not."

Dad continued. "Say you find that each customer likes a different feel of finish. From a functional point of view, both tools are exactly the same and so is even the look of the finish. But imagine that one customer likes a softer feel for the finish than the other. Maybe it stems from a difference in their personalities or just simply a matter of taste. But it doesn't really matter. What matters is that you are aware of it, you are sensitive to this unique aspect, and above all you make a good note of it.

"You must memorize it, so the next time they ask for a service you pull out this information," Dad explained. "You verify again, adjust a little and now you have a loyal customer. That's what makes the difference between an okay service and a very special one. By the way Steve, I like your DNA approach."

Dad asked Steve not to stay at work for too long, wished him a good night, and hung up the phone.

Steve breathed a sigh of relief. "I guess I was not that far off with my concept. Dad probably remembers every customer and their unique personalities. It is as though he has instant access to a data bank of all our customers' DNA. With just a few simple questions he can modify any service to exactly match every customer's needs—using his brain data bank and his craftsmanship knowledge."

Steve got up and walked toward the door connecting the office to the shop. "It's a good time to wrap things up," he thought while locking the door. "Not only has Dad confirmed my intuition, but I learned something new. It is how Dad uses his customer's DNA data bank at the very early stage of receiving the order. As he gets a service request, he immediately personalizes it to the customer in a way that reflects his unique aspects. It's as if he has a written customer profile in his head that he attaches to every order."

Satisfied, Steve was ready to call it a night. He again began to collect his belongings. "I have made a lot of progress during the past hours…"

Then it hit him. "There is still a big problem! It is all in Dad's head—and I'm not sure I have enough time to capture it all."

Yet, there was another bothersome thought. It wasn't Dad who had made the cut-off call.

Transforming Insights to Actions

Steve put his stuff back for the third time that night. The nagging thought about the mysterious phone call didn't leave him, but there was little he could do about it.

Yet he could have dealt with the other alarming problem—the customer DNA data bank. "I have to find how to transform the idea into a working methodology, and it has to begin tomorrow," he concluded. "I must figure out a way to extract all our customers' DNA knowledge from Dad's head before it's too late. Otherwise, with his upcoming departure, I will quickly lose the major asset that allows us to succeed."

Steve walked back and forth in the small office. His mind was going a million miles an hour, searching for a way to transform his insights into actions. Then he stopped. "That's it! I need to draw out the information that Dad stores in his head into a system, which I can use on an ongoing basis long after he retires. I'm sure that together we can come up with a simple way to do it.

"With that we will be able to put each customer's DNA into a solid form. As to the professional aspect of doing the service, we have that knowledge with our loyal workers, and I believe that over time I will be able to gain enough confidence in this aspect as well."

Steve put a headline on his second page, and under it he wrote:

To - Do checklist :

- Develop DNA information format

- Get our customers' DNA data from Dad

- Store in a quick access system

- Attach a DNA profile to every order

Steve was restless. He knew that the distance between concepts and application is always very far. It is hard enough to come up with a new concept, but it is much harder to bring it to life.

"The first item on the list—of developing an information format—is something Dad and I can do within a few hours," he thought. "But the second one, of getting Dad's data bank, would be much harder. Not only would it take a great deal of effort to articulate Dad's knowledge, but it would be just as hard to cover every single one of our customers. Completing the task is likely to take too long."

For a moment Steve felt that he was stuck, but his college education seemed to pay off once more. "I can use the 80/20 rule in order to expedite things," he thought. "Instead of going through all of our customers, we can look at the few who account for most of our sales. I bet the principle developed by the Italian economist Pareto—where in many cases 80% of the result comes from only 20% of the source—can be applied to us as well. We better start from top to bottom. At first we will analyze only the customers who give us the most business, and then we will move on to the others to make it more manageable."

He then added to his to-do list:

- Set priorities:

  For top three customers first,

  and for the rest, downwards in descending order.

"After we have figured out the DNA of our top three customers, we can move on to the other action item on the list—the storage of the data into a quick access system," Steve thought. "We can start with a simple manual filing and storing system and convert it to a computerized one later on. Meanwhile, we can attach our top three customers' DNA profiles to their orders. Then, we can gradually deal with the rest of our customers in a similar manner.

Not only did he have a good focused checklist, but Steve felt he had a good approach with set priorities from top to bottom.

Satisfied, he sat down on Dad's chair and put his feet on the desk. He closed his eyes for a couple of minutes. The short rest made him realize that something was missing in his plan.

Fragmented Relations and Service Ratio

Steve looked again at his two pages. His eyes were moving back and forth trying to see if his action list covered his insights. Right then and there, he discovered the missing part.

"My plan only deals with the customer's DNA aspect. However, what about the other important part of implementing it along the entire service cycle? How would I do it from the customer request, all the way through delivering the service? In fact, I don't even know how to do it for our top three clients."

Steve decided that no matter how late it was he wouldn't leave the office. He re-examined his checklist. "Tomorrow I can develop with Dad, our top-of-the-list customers' DNA profile. But adjusting it to the customers, especially when they are not present, is a whole different ball game. In his head, Dad does it at the very beginning of receiving the order. But how does he do it for the rest of the cycle?"

For the next few minutes Steve wrestled with the question and could not come to any conclusion. He was trying to envision how it could be done for a single customer. The fact that their business provided service indirectly, made it even more complicated.

He continued to struggle with the issue, and doubts were creeping into his mind. "If this is difficult to do for a single customer, what do you do when you have many? Maybe that is a major obstacle that even Dad doesn't know how to overcome."

He reached for the phone and began dialing Dad, but immediately stopped. It was too late to call.

"I guess I have to resolve it on my own," he thought. He went back to Dad's example of the hairdresser. "A successful hairdresser has the natural ability to develop and store her customer's DNA in her head. Then she can utilize it throughout the service cycle—from the moment of setting up an appointment, through waiting at the hair salon, having the treatment, and leaving, until the next time. It is as if she interacts with her customer continuously.

"However our cycles are different. We interact with our customer in a fragmented way, just as Sharon did with Amos."

He paused. "But how fragmented is it?"

That brought other service providers to mind. "The painter, the plumber, the electrician, the fire sprinkler systems installer, the parts manufacturer, their cycles are fragmented as well. What can you do when it is the nature of your service?"

Steve went back and forth, analyzing other examples. He was comparing the indirect to the direct service world, fragmented to continuous cycles, customers to service providers, personal attention to satisfaction...and the words were starting to lose any rational meaning. He felt as though there was a blender inside his head, mixing it all up at an increasing speed, to the point where nothing made sense anymore.

"If I want to avoid losing it all, I better change from water to coffee. Thank goodness I had the instinct to keep my thoughts on paper while my mind was still fresh and clear."

Steve went to pour himself a cup of coffee, but there were only muddy leftovers at the bottom of the pot. He decided he might as well brew a fresh one.

"I better stretch for a few minutes until the coffee is done," he thought, and all of a sudden everything clicked. "It is all about time. Not the time to go home, at least not yet. It is the time dimension of the cycle."

Steve's mind quickly went back to the hairdresser example with the two blonde ladies. "How long does it take to finish the job? It shouldn't really matter to the hairdresser whose DNA she likes better—the bubbly or the introverted one. If she wants to be successful for either one, she needs to tailor her service according to the customer DNA—and it would probably take the same amount of time."

He then used his analytical skills and experience as a customer to evaluate the time elements.

"It is likely that each service cycle would take about two hours from start to finish. But I wonder how long the customer isn't receiving any attention?

"Hairstyling and getting personal attention while waiting, probably amounts to about eighty percent of the overall service cycle," he estimated.

"It really means that the customer would be waiting only twenty percent of the two hours without getting any attention. It is only a little bit over a twenty minute wait; and for some ladies it may be even too short to enjoy a beauty magazine."

Steve made a sketch to depict his idea:

Looking at sketch Steve continued, "Eighty percent may be a fair figure for the hairdresser and the like who belong to the direct service world.

But what about us, the indirect service providers? What is the percentage of our customer interaction during the entire service cycle?

"I don't have solid data to calculate our ratio, but I bet it is much lower than the eighty percent mark. The smaller the figure is, the less interaction we have with our customer. What is even worse, the customer has no idea what is really happening with his order—unless he calls us."

And then it hit home. "That's exactly what happened with Sharon and Amos.

"How long was she kept in the dark regarding her order? How much frustration did she have, not knowing when her order would arrive? She was promised her sofa delivery to be in four weeks and got it after six and a half weeks instead. I wonder what would have happened if she hadn't called Amos almost every day after the assumed delivery date. Maybe the sofa would have been delivered in nine weeks."

He tried to compare the time Sharon was served directly to the overall length of service cycle for her sofa. "Sharon only received personal attention in the very beginning and at the end when the sofa was delivered.

"If I count the time Amos was at the house, Sharon's time at Amos's shop and finally at delivery, it can't be more than two days all together. I will not count her fruitless time spent on numerous follow-up calls to Amos—that was sheer frustration.

"The total service cycle from Amos's initial visit to sofa delivery was six and a half weeks. So there was no more than two days, in which there was direct interaction, out of a forty-five day cycle. That is only about four percent. Sharon was kept in the dark for ninety-six percent of the cycle."

And then it dawned on Steve that he had discovered a new way of measuring service efficiency—*service ratio*! Amos's service ratio was only four percent. It was mind-boggling.

The more Steve thought about it, the more he was concerned with their situation. He could not conclude what their service ratio might be, but he could picture what a four percent would do to a hairstyling business.

"I can't even imagine what the reaction would be of the two blonde ladies in the hair salon, if they had to experience a four percent service efficiency. It is as if they had been waiting close to fifty hours to get their hair done. That would definitely create a harmonious relationship between them and the hairdresser," Steve thought facetiously.

"In such an erroneous situation, it wouldn't take long before they got into a fight—totally frustrated with each other, suggesting settling the matter outside," he concluded,

And he imagined the blonde ladies and the hairdresser fighting in a mud-wrestling competition where he, Amos, Dad, and Sharon were amongst the cheering audience. "Mom would never watch such a competition," he thought, chuckling to himself.

A Dinghy and a Speedboat Race

Coming back to reality from the mud wrestling imaginary scene, a four percent service ratio was too disturbing for Steve.

"A successful hairdresser has a ratio of about eighty percent. Amos was at four percent and maybe we are as well. How could there be such a huge gap between us and her? It is as if we're both in the low performance boat, and the hairdresser is in the high performance one."

He couldn't come up with a good explanation, but in his mind Steve could depict another scene where he and Amos were rowing a dinghy, chasing the hairdresser's speedboat in a race on the "customer satisfaction river." Falling behind, as they pushed to increase their rowing speed, he could imagine them both yelling, "Please let us know what it takes to be like you!"

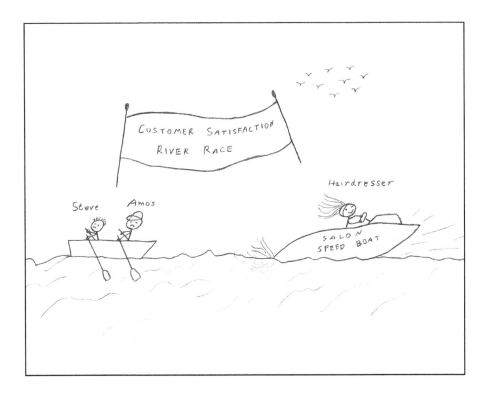

The small office, the late hour, and the fact that he suddenly realized how hungry he was made him wonder, "Maybe it is not our boats that make the difference? Perhaps we simply race in different waters."

He went back to his imaginary boat racing scene. "That's it! The hairdresser is in the direct service world and that's why she has a short cycle. That is where she is sailing. It must be the major reason for her high percentage service ratio. She has short service cycles but ours are long."

He wondered if this was the case with other direct service providers. Visiting a doctor came first to his mind. "How long does it take?" Steve thought. "Is it fifteen minutes or perhaps a little bit more? It probably wouldn't last more than half an hour."

Then others popped into his head. "A psychologist, a voice coach, a physiotherapist, a manicurist, and the like—how long would it take there?"

Running their processes in his mind, he concluded, "Their service cycles are measured by the hour and sometimes even shorter. Occasionally, you receive service in a matter of a few minutes. However, in our indirect world the service cycle is usually longer, and measured by days or even weeks. So, our river is different by its nature than that of the hairdresser and direct services alike."

It seemed that Steve had found a solid correlation, yet the outlook was gloomy.

"Is it possible that the nature of the indirect service world dictates a very low service ratio, with only a few percentage of customer interaction during a long cycle? And is that why it is so difficult to satisfy our customers? Is it true that the longer the cycle is, the more fragmented it becomes?"

It was almost like a mathematical equation. "Long service cycles result in a poor service ratio and poor customer satisfaction. Short cycles are the opposite.... But are they really?"

Bye Customers in Fast Lanes

11:30 p.m.

Steve was getting tired, and above all he was very hungry. He had not had anything but water and coffee since lunch. He got off his chair and searched the small cabinet at the corner of the office, hoping to find something to eat. He then walked to the kitchenette outside, and there was nothing left—not even a cookie. The nearby twenty-four-hour store came to mind.

He put on his coat and stepped outside the office. Driving his car, he was at the store in just a matter of minutes. The store was almost empty, with only one person at the cash register paying for gas. Steve wandered around a little and eventually decided to get a sandwich. The only thing he could find was a cold wrapped one. "I can just heat it up at the office," he decided. He grabbed some milk and cookies too.

As he was getting ready to leave, the store seemed a little busier. There were a few more people shopping around. Standing in line were five people ahead of him, waiting for the lethargic cashier. Steve patiently waited to pay, and it took him about ten minutes before he was back in his car.

"There was only one person in line when I came in," Steve thought while driving. "I expected the store to be empty this late and next thing I know, there were five people ahead in line. The service was a bit slow. It took longer than I expected, probably because the cashier had some problems processing credit card payments. I'm glad I paid in cash. I guess Murphy's Law—suggesting that anything that can possibly go wrong will go wrong—works at night as well."

Back in his office he prepared some coffee, toasted his sandwich, sat in his chair and ate.

"Well, it's not a gourmet meal, but it definitely does the job," he thought.

Now feeling satisfied, he could get back to business. His visit to the store had triggered a totally different view—of short cycle services.

"We, as indirect service providers, have a low percentage service ratio with fragmented long cycles. They have short cycles with a high ratio of...." Steve stopped right there. His conclusion about speedy direct service with high service ratio and customer satisfaction was falling apart.

"I just left a place with a short service cycle, and it was fragmented as well—in fact maybe too fragmented! From the moment I walked in until I left, the only time I got attention was at the cash register; and I'm not sure I should even count it. The cashier was slothful and far from welcoming. He was just doing his job and nothing else. An automatic cashier machine would have probably done a better job. Maybe he deserves *zero* percent service efficiency?

"Maybe I'm too harsh," Steve thought, and re-calculated more graciously his entire service cycle at the twenty-four-hour store. "It took me about ten minutes to walk around, get my stuff, and join the line. Then I was waiting in line for around ten more minutes, including a minute to pay. So the total service cycle was approximately twenty minutes with one minute of direct service. Only one minute over twenty—that's a five percent service ratio. It's unbelievable that such a short cycle can be so inefficient and fragmented."

He quickly drew a sketch depicting his experience at the store:

But Steve didn't stop there. He visualized the twenty-four-hour store scene even further "What would have happened if someone had to ask for help in finding something? How quickly would he or she get service from the cashier? What would have happened in the meanwhile to the line of people waiting to pay, while the cashier would be assisting others? I bet the service ratio would be even below the five percent. I would probably just have walked out and left for the other store nearby."

Provoked by his discovery of highly fragmented direct service, Steve was searching for other examples of short cycles. The first thing that came to mind was the retail business. "There, the cycles are usually short. Not by the hours, but by the minutes. You come in, you look around, and if you find what you want, you pay at the cash register. If you don't find anything, you leave. It feels quick and smooth. But is the cycle really any different from the twenty-four-hour store?"

He thought of his experience in large department stores. "How long did the process last? How many times, if any, did I get personal attention that would make me feel special during the cycle before I made the purchase? How often was I offered help after I was already getting frustrated? And how many times did I leave the store empty-handed?"

He then continued, "How long does it take to lose patience and walk away, when you don't find what you want, or when nobody comes around to help? Is it five or ten minutes? It probably wouldn't take longer than that. So what we have here is a sequence of events that usually happen in a matter of minutes, yet the cycle can become highly fragmented, with very poor service results."

It became clear that these situations happened more often than not. Steve was convinced that as a customer, he was not alone. And he then came to a realization which was rather disturbing.

"It looks as though there are two main types of service cycles," he carried on. "One that ends with a 'buy' and the other that ends with a 'bye'.

"In the buy cycle, the customer usually receives more direct interaction from the store personnel. The bye cycle is shorter and abrupt. Typically it ends when the customer just walks away frustrated. More often than not, it's because he or she were given very little attention, if any. After all, you wouldn't have walked in unless you had an initial interest to buy something.

"I wonder if anyone ever measured the number of bye customers versus the number of the buy customers during a single day. Perhaps there's a correlation to a low service ratio. Is there a measurement as to how much business is being lost in such cases? If the loss of a bye customer is bad enough, what is the real damage when the word of a customer's frustration spreads around?

"Maybe service providers just need to take a sample and ask customers at the store exit if they are a bye customer. As awkward as it may sound, it could provide an idea as to the magnitude of the problem."

The whole concept of fragmented service cycles, service ratio percentages, and the notion of bye customers versus buy ones shook Steve up.

"I bet if I take a fifteen- to twenty-minute typical buying cycle, and break it into a minute-by-minute process, I will find that the service ratio is closer to Amos's than that of the hairdresser.

"So fast lane businesses that have a service cycle of minutes may have a horrifyingly low service ratio, which can yield too many bye customers. What is even scarier is that most service providers are not even aware of it."

Dichotomy Medals and a Strange Dream

Although it was after midnight, the toasted sandwich and the fresh coffee recharged Steve. The increased sugar level and caffeine in his blood pumped him up.

Fragmented direct service, with surprisingly low efficiency, brought another scene into his mind. Steve envisioned a Saturday's shopping fun: Long waits at the cashier, with heavy bags in tow, when a typical fifteen minutes buying cycle could be doubled or tripled—and the service ratio efficiency deteriorates.

This view and his experience at the twenty-four hour store with its lethargic cashier, made him think about their service shop.

"Do we get sluggish as well from time to time?" Steve asked himself. "I wonder if we have bye customers too? Maybe we are not at the bottom of the list, but I still need to find a way so that we will not fall into the same trap."

Steve paused for a moment. "I don't know what our service ratio is and how much better it could be. But a four percent ratio is totally unacceptable—it's as if you lose the race before even starting it."

Thinking about his service grading method in Sharon's experience with Amos, he continued. "Even an F grade seems too high for a four percent service ratio. But what about our customers, and how do they grade us? Do I have any data to tell me where we are? Maybe we are not at four percent, but I'm not sure we are much higher than that."

Steve softened his stance a bit. "Well, maybe I'm too tough on Amos. After all, Sharon approached him based on Dad's recommendation of his professional abilities. Maybe like Amos, we think we give the best service, but perhaps our customers don't hold the same view."

He then tried to figure out their service ratio, and concluded with a smile. "If it is as low as I think, our customers must love us—or maybe it is our craftsmanship that keeps them with us. At least no customer has asked us, yet, to face him in a mud-wrestling fight."

He then continued. "It may very well be that good craftsmanship, with an unknowingly low service ratio, is more common than not. Perhaps our competitors are in the same boat. However, what would happen if one day a new competitor stepped in and not only excelled in workmanship, but also developed a better service efficiency?

Steve chuckled to himself. "I bet it wouldn't be long before I found myself partnering with Amos. It will be a Steve and Amos Dichotomy. At least Amos will not feel lonely out there for too long. We would probably be like gold and silver medalists in the Olympics, standing on the podium, arguing about who should have won the dichotomy gold medal. Meanwhile, the new competitor would be grabbing the rest of the medals for the entire games."

Steve did not know if he was becoming more open with self-criticism or more creative in his sense of humor—or if it was simply because of the late hour. He was getting very tired, and even the coffee couldn't stop him from dozing off.

It is in moments like these, when you are still somewhat awake and have a lot of things running through your mind, though not in the most logical order. Your eyelids are getting heavier, and you are ready to fall asleep.

A flurry of images rattled around in Steve's mind: Dad talking about tools as living people, spiraling service cycles, customers' DNA attached to paper orders, Sharon talking to the hairdresser, poor service ratio and competitors chasing him and Amos.

Then his head hit the table.

Mr. Bupti

The impact of Steve's head on the table didn't awaken him. His head lay at an awkward angle, yet it didn't disturb him—until the phone rang. It was an abrupt end to a strange dream. He jumped off his chair and reached for the phone, which was placed at the other end of the table. But by the time he had grabbed it, the ringing had stopped. Frustrated, he rubbed his stiff neck and stretched. Just as he was ready to go and wash his face, the phone rang again. Quickly he picked up the phone, and there was a faint background noise. But this time he could hear the voice on the other side.

"Hello I am Mr. Bupti, from the Bupti Service Company, can I speak with the owner?" he asked.

Steve glanced at his watch to discover it was almost one o'clock in the morning. His head wasn't entirely clear from the dream, and the unusual time for a call made him hesitate for a while.

"Hello, Hello, is anybody there? Can I please talk to the owner?" Mr. Bupti asked again with his distinct accent.

"Well, he is not around, but I am the owner's son," Steve replied.

"Ahhh, so maybe I can talk to you instead?" Mr. Bupti suggested.

"It is after midnight here, but maybe I can help," Steve said. After all he was soon to take the lead in the company.

"I am so sorry, I must have miscalculated the time difference between our continents," Mr. Bupti replied. "I tried earlier but couldn't get through. Should I call tomorrow?"

"Well, since we are already talking, why don't you go ahead," Steve answered as his curiosity peaked.

"I have relatives living in your area, and your reputation is well known," Mr. Bupti said and paused.

Using the break Steve interjected, "Thanks for the compliment. Would they be interested in our services?"

"Not exactly that," Mr. Bupti said. "In my country our company provides similar services to yours, amongst a few other things. Maybe we can do business together?"

Mr. Bupti hesitated slightly and then continued, "There have been rumors that your company is having financial difficulties. Maybe it is up for sale? We are looking to expand our activities, along with acquiring the best knowledge around. So maybe we can work something out."

There was a moment of silence. "Mr. Bupti, I think you really need to talk to my father," Steve replied. The proposition had caught him entirely by surprise.

"Is there a way I can talk to him directly?" Mr. Bupti asked. "I promise to call during the day, and I apologize again for my mistake in calculating the hour. I guarantee to keep it all confidential."

Steve gave Mr. Bupti Dad's personal phone number and they finished the call.

Steve was totally shaken. Not just by the odd hour and Mr. Bupti's call, but by the possibility that their business may have a bigger problem than he ever imagined. Suddenly his vision of a new competitor grabbing all the gold medals, didn't seem so far out.

"Rumors going around can worsen any situation," he thought. "I must bring it up with Dad."

Steve would have called Dad right away, but it was far too late; and there were other things to explore before he talked to him.

Challenging the Imagination

1:00 a.m.

Still shaken at the turn of events, Steve realized he had not taken Mr. Bupti's phone number—nor did he have any other information about him. He wasn't even sure how the name was spelled. Because of the late hour and the looming challenges ahead, he decided not to go through an elaborate search. His intuition was telling him it was unnecessary; and also that Mr. Bupti could be a serious contender.

As eager as he was to share everything with Dad, he had to wait until the morning. It was very late and Steve was extremely weary. Yet, with the prospect of a serious threat, he felt the urgency to continue with his plan to transform insights into actions.

"If we do it right, we will become the competitor who chases the others, armed with the best quality and service efficiency," he concluded.

Steve went through his various pages to refocus his thoughts. He re-read his notes on his to-do list and then realized that he must add another key item. With his new view of service and the notion of bye customers, he wrote:

○ ***Must find what our service ratio is***

He looked at his note, but he wasn't sure how to calculate the ratio. He searched through his other papers, and the service ratio sketches were in front. "Analyzing the hairdresser service process and the twenty-four-hour store, is what helped me in finding their efficiency. I must do it for our business as well."

Now charged up, he was ready for the task. Then his eyes caught sight of Sharon's photo which he kept on the desk. He realized how much time had passed since he had spoken with her. It was far too late to call. "I'm sure she will understand why I forgot to wish her good night," he mumbled.

As he was thinking of Sharon, an idea clicked. "Maybe before analyzing our service, I should review Amos's process. Anyway, I already did most of the ground work. Besides re-calculating more accurately his service ratio, I can do it with a new twist. If I take Sharon's sofa experience and try to fix the flaws in it, I may find a method for process improvement. It might give me the answers of how to do it in our situation and improve our service efficiency as well.

He glanced at Sharon's photo. "I wish Sharon was sitting with me right now, helping me to dissect exactly what has transpired." But Sharon was already asleep and Steve was sitting alone in his office.

"I guess I have to do it all by myself," he thought. "Even though Amos and I are dichotomy partners, in the case of the sofa, he was the service provider and we were the customers. Being closely involved, I can represent Sharon in an unbiased way. Can I write for Amos my insights along with a check-list of things for him to do, as a virtual simulation?"

Steve tried to put the key elements of his insights into the sofa saga: Sharon's customer DNA, her sofa specifications, quality, and time requirements. He decided to dissect the entire process from the very beginning all the way to its end, looking at every step that Amos could have taken to provide his best service and make Sharon feel special.

He grabbed another piece of paper and started writing his summary of the key events as he remembered them.

It was not long before the paper was covered with many notes. Instead of becoming clearer, it turned out to be rather confusing. "It is like not seeing the forest for its trees," he said, folding the paper into a small ball and tossing it toward the waste basket at the far end corner of the office. Of course he missed.

"During the day I never miss. Even the most logical person might lose clarity when emotions, time limits and late nights are involved," Steve muttered as he justified his failure.

He tried again to put his thoughts in a sensible order.

"I don't like the outcome of my events capturing. What can I do to encapsulate the important elements of the story while not being submerged in unnecessary details?" he wondered.

He decided to take a step back and reorganize his thought process. After all, he was an analytical person with a distinguished business degree.

Instead of writing notes depicting the story at random, he decided to make a bulleted list where he would describe the key events and organize them in a timeline.

Steve tried to crystallize in his mind where the first interaction with Amos had really happened. He wrote on paper a little note, *Sharon calling on Amos*. He then drew a little telephone depicting Sharon's call. To illustrate the next step, he drew Amos's truck arriving at their house. He then carried on, charting the whole process—numbering its key steps. It was like taking a journey along the river-flow of Sharon's sofa saga—all the way from the very beginning to the end.

Instead of making a bulleted list of the key events, Steve found himself dealing with a new form of art, at least new for him: the art of describing a whole complicated story with one plain chart. "Sharon would laugh at my childish drawing, but I don't intend to share it with her just yet."

He looked at his chart and he was very pleased with his masterpiece. "I could have drowned in all of the small details rather than just seeing the simple picture."

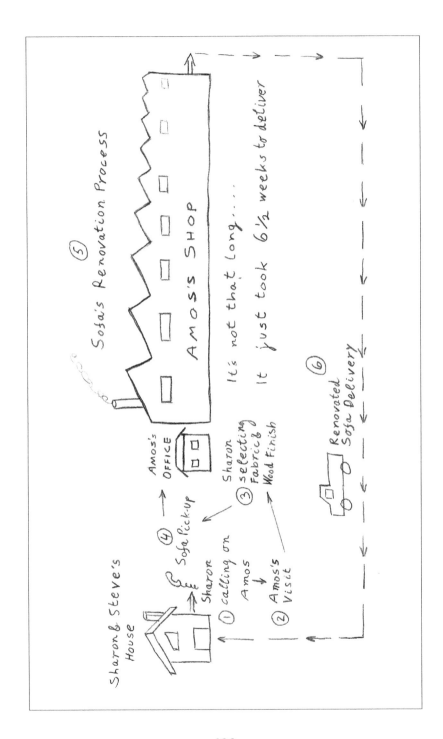

Sofa's Renovation Process

Sharon & Steve's House

① calling on Amos

② Amos's Visit

③ Sharon selecting Fabric & Wood Finish

④ Sofa Pickup

Amos's Office

⑤ Amos's Shop

It's not that long......

It just took 6½ weeks to deliver

⑥ Renovated Sofa Delivery

Steve then thought of ideas that could have improved the situation. He envisioned the events like a movie. Images of how things had occurred and how each event could be simplified and improved upon, ran through his mind.

He started with the very first step, when Sharon had called Amos. He was not there to listen to the exact details of how the conversation had transpired: how Amos had answered the call, what he had said, and what he had done.

And then Sharon's DNA jumped into his mind.

"During the phone conversation, right there at the very beginning, that is where the process had just started and that is when the customer DNA concept should have been initiated. One does not have the order yet, but the interaction with the customer has already begun. The cycle did not start at Amos's visit. It really started earlier, when Sharon called Amos.

"At the end of his conversation with Sharon, Amos could have asked himself how she was on the phone. Was she friendly, outgoing, polite, dry, distant, demanding? Does she want to move on with her project, and what might be my next step? Is there anything in her personality that I can detect and capture while it is still fresh?

"It could have been Amos's first opportunity to make a note of his impression of a potential customer and store it in a designated file," Steve noted. "By doing so, the customer DNA could actually be defined right from the start, while the mind is clear and totally focused on the conversation—before turning to the next job on the hot list."

Steve was on a roll. "From that point on, Amos could have added more insights of Sharon and her special requirements along the cycle—like the importance of meeting the delivery date. While upgrading his initial impression of her customer DNA, he could have acted accordingly to meet her full expectations."

Steve felt as though he had the ability to change the script and the outcome by improving the process.

"Amos also could have kept her informed of the sofa renovation progress throughout the entire process of his work. By doing so, he could have substantially improved his four percent service ratio. It could have turned the entire situation around, and made both Sharon and Amos happy with their business relationship—then, and in the future."

With this, Steve was ready to move forward but he stopped there. He looked at his sketch with new insight, "So a charting technique can be utilized as a tool for analyzing any process. From there, changing the situation is limited only by your imagination."

Oscillating Chart on Top of Articles

Without looking at his watch Steve knew it was getting very late. He was beyond tired. Physically and emotionally drained, he was ready to wrap things up and finally get himself home to bed.

He stood up and looked at his notes. Nagging thoughts of the upcoming challenges and financial liabilities were going through his mind. All of his newly discovered insights were in front of him. "Dad is going to retire soon and there is so much to do," he thought. "I learned modesty as a key value and what real craftsmanship is. I found out what customer DNA is, and the need to adjust to it throughout the entire service cycle. I learned how, in spite of good intentions, things can go wrong—just as they did between Amos and Sharon. I discovered how to grade service performance, both from the customer and service provider's perspective. I found out what *service ratio* is and defined 'bye' customers too. I even found a way to draw the process of a service cycle—with the key steps involved—and how to improve the flow of events. But above all I am overtly tired now and just want to go home."

As he began to collect his things, he noticed another chart on the table. It was a financial chart, titled in Dad's hand writing- "Sales over Ten Years." He had seen quarterly and annual data, but never before had he seen a ten-year view of their business.

"I wonder what prompted Dad to prepare this chart. Was he trying to summarize the last ten years as part of the information requested by the bank, or was it for something else?"

Steve looked closer at the sales chart and noticed that it had yesterday's date on it. The sales information showed an unexpected view. The average sales trend line was almost flat, indicating that the business did not really grow over the last decade. However, the sales line itself was not a straight line. It had some ups and some downs, with a pattern like a far away mountain skyline view.

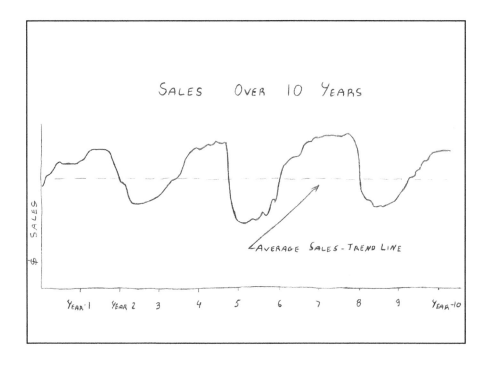

As Steve looked closely at the chart, he noticed it was placed over some business magazines stacked on top of each other in a precise order—a reflection of Dad's personality. He looked through the pile, glancing first at the title on the front cover of each magazine. They were about tool servicing, new equipment, new technologies, accounting principles, and more. But the one cover that grabbed his attention most was titled, "On Cycles and Bottlenecks." He opened the magazine and started reading.

Steve never made it home that night. He ended up groggily dragging himself to the customer's couch, situated near the entrance of the office. Holding the article in his hands, he fell asleep sometime around three o'clock that morning.

MYSTERIOUS PATTERNS

A Walk Around the Block

5:00 a.m.

When Steve woke up two hours later, his head was heavy, his neck was cramped, and he was still holding the article. He put it aside and decided to take a short walk around the building just to stretch his body and clear his mind. Another long day was waiting for him, and he knew that he was going to have a lengthy discussion with Dad. There were a lot of issues to resolve.

The fresh morning air and fast-paced power walk sped up Steve's breathing and quickly got his mind back on track. He tried to put together the key things he had read in the article. It was a short article, only a few pages long. It used terms that were not entirely clear: "cycles and the pendulum," about "bottleneck dynamics," and "boundaries" amongst others. They sounded a bit academic.

They reminded Steve of one of the most disliked classes he had taken in college. He could not figure out its exact name but he remembered it as "advanced business algorithms in a stochastic world." Most people cannot even comprehend what that means.

But in the article, there was not a hint of advanced mathematics, not even basic math. It was written in a simple way and told about real life experience. Although the terms were somewhat ambiguous, Steve felt that they presented common sense, which could intuitively be connected to their company.

It must have been the cool morning air and the fast pace that caused Steve to see things in a multidimensional order. Maybe it was simply his body's reaction to little sleep and the immediate challenge in front of him.

Whatever it was, it inspired Steve to have a crystal clear vision of three different floating clusters. In one he envisioned his insight pages with notes about customer DNA, service cycles, an implementation plan, the notion of direct and indirect service, fragmented relations, and service ratio—all forming one chapter of knowledge to be further explored. In the second cluster was the article, "On Cycles and Bottlenecks," with its vague yet intuitively familiar terms, waiting to be discovered. In the third cluster was his father's chart with its unexplainable pattern.

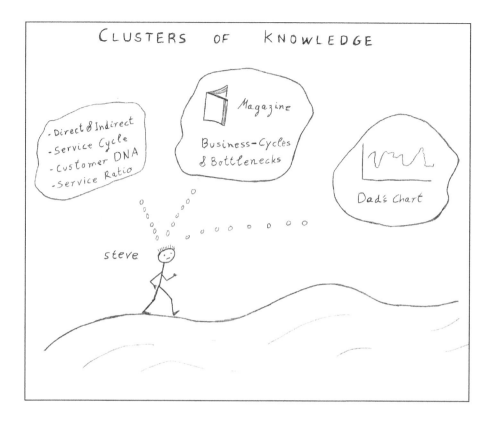

It was the inner voice of Steve's intuition suggesting that the three clusters were interconnected.

"I should have a good go with the first one," he said. "But the other clusters only show a glimpse of their true essence, hiding two more chapters of knowledge to learn—and that is where I have to focus my energy. I better do it with Dad's help."

With this vision still in sight, he thought, "I should learn them all." But the one that challenged him the most was the least understood—the third cluster with Dad's chart.

Is It Seasonality?

The town was built on undulating land, and the shop was located on the top of a small hill. Its surrounding streets presented a challenge for fast walkers. Steve was walking uphill at a fast pace, and with the vivid image of the clusters in his mind he pictured Dad's chart with its peaks and valleys.

"I thought our business was pretty solid. With Dad's excellent reputation, I was convinced that over the years it was steadily growing. Instead the chart showed it was rather flat. Is that the reason why we have issues with the bank—along with the tightening economy situation? To complicate things even further, out of nowhere I get this strange call from Mr. Bupti. It seems that word is spreading. I should definitely clarify it with Dad."

On this note, a thought crossed his mind, "Maybe Dad was surprised as well. He might have left his chart on the table for us to discuss its pattern and implications."

Instead of waiting to check it with Dad, Steve was trying to understand what might have caused this irregular pattern. "Is it possible that we have ups and downs due to other reasons, as in seasonality, or is it something else?

"I wonder what may be a good example...." The *clothing industry* was the first thing that leaped to his mind. "I have no experience in this field except from being a customer. Yet acting as a customer, and having the outside view already proved its advantage."

Steve had already discovered the customer cycle and the notion of a bye customer at department stores. Striding up the hill, he was now ready to explore different type of cycles. Not only that of a customer—from walking in, all the way to leaving—but of cycles that are created by weather and seasons, which affect the entire service enterprise.

With this view in mind, he thought, "I can imagine how seasons have an effect on customer demand in a cyclical manner. Every transition from one season to another must bring large swings in sales; and a lot of pressure for the people who work around it. So what does it take—changing from winter to spring?"

As he was quickly pacing up the hill, he made in his head a list of the tasks: Purchasing of new goods, storing old ones, moving things around, displaying them, reorganizing everything, and of course selling them. He had a few more. Instead of memorizing them, he decided he would write them down when he got back to the office.

He then thought, "Maybe I should utilize the charting technique to depict the process instead? That would allow a clearer view."

And his thoughts drifted back to the seasonality cycles. "It happens again in transitioning from spring to summer, from summer to autumn, from autumn to winter and all over again from winter to spring. On and on go the cycles, all in a regular pattern."

In Steve's mind, he was picturing a wave with a repeating pattern of low and high tides, swinging from one season to another, year after year in a steady motion.

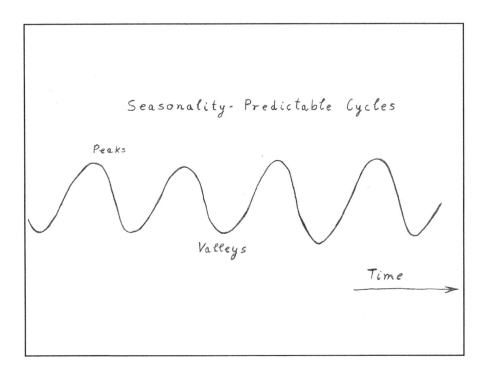

But Dad's chart was far from being steady. He felt something was missing.

"The picture I have in mind is not complete. The steady wave motion seems to oversimplify our situation." He shook his head to clear his thoughts, and suddenly a new idea crossed his mind.

"Holidays—that's what's missing in understanding the big picture. They come on top of seasonal cycles, usually with higher intensity in their up-turn and then in the downturn. So even stable cycles, could be disrupted by the impact of other cycles—altogether yielding an erratic situation. Is this what we have?"

As he was striding up and down the hill, he was deep in thought, trying to understand the evolving cycles of seasons and holidays together. "I wonder if they have a similar pattern to Dad's chart, or will I get something else completely?"

He tried to depict the combined outcome. "Seasons happen in a regular manner, so I can probably draw them the same way year in and year out. Holidays occur regularly every year as well, but with a higher intensity and different timing. I can draw each on a different paper. If I put the two pages on top of each other, I can marry them into one chart, probably making a new pattern made of two different repetitive cycles—with much sharper swings from high to low."

In his mind he tried to visualize it. "When I get back to the office, I will make that chart," he thought. "Once I finish, I will compare it to the one Dad left on top of the articles, to see if there is any resemblance between the two. Maybe it will explain what happened with our business."

Drawing in Waves

6:00 a.m.

The sound of a Harley Davidson driving by at full throttle pulled Steve out of his deep thoughts. He looked at his watch and couldn't believe how a ten-minute walk had turned into a full hour. He found himself standing in front of their shop entrance. Steve wondered how many times he may have circled around in one hour. He just hoped nobody had noticed his detached expression, thinking about clusters and chapters of knowledge and very nearly banging into a lamp post. He pushed straight through the office door, grabbed a paper, and started to jot down his idea of cycles.

He looked closely at his chart to make sure he had drawn the seasonality wave-line in a consistent manner. "I think Dad will be surprised with my analysis. Probably with the passage of time I am becoming a better artist, at least at drawing charts," Steve thought, smiling.

He took out a second page for drawing the holiday cycles, and as he was doing so, Dad walked into the office.

"Hey, good morning son," he said. "When did you get in? I was in the office a few minutes ago and it was empty."

"Actually I didn't get in, I stayed all night," Steve replied. "I just took a walk around the block to get some fresh air—that's probably why you didn't see me."

Dad was ready to lecture Steve for staying up all night, but Steve continued talking. He began telling Dad about what he had been through since their telephone conversation the previous night.

Dad interrupted him. "You probably want to tell me more about your customer DNA, but I bet you've had nothing to eat since yesterday's lunch. Instead of us talking here, let's go and have breakfast at Jim's place."

Dad's old friend, Jim, was an owner of a restaurant just a few blocks away from their shop.

"Breakfast sounds great," Steve answered. "I only had a midnight snack from the twenty-four hour store down the street. I had to wait long in line to pay a sluggish cashier, and it helped me realize that our service isn't that bad."

Steve then stood up. "And Dad, I want to talk about our customer DNA and I prepared a whole plan for it. But before we analyze our customers, we may need to explore what is going on with our own business DNA and its odd cycles. I must tell you about a strange phone call I received in the middle of the night—so much has transpired since we last talked."

He paused. "By the way Dad, did you deliberately leave your ten-year chart on the desk for me to see, or is it confidential information for the bank?"

Dad could tell Steve was very excited and kept himself from responding. After all, he could identify with sleepless nights and skipping meals at frustrating times.

Steve picked up his insights pages, his action checklist, and his sketches. Dad took his chart, along with the magazines, and off they went to have breakfast—one of the longest they would ever have.

Table Manners and Reading Magazines

It took only a few minutes to get to Jim's restaurant. Along the way their conversation was casual. As tempted as Steve was to further question Dad about their situation with the bank, and also tell him about rumors spreading around and Mr. Bupti, he decided to bring it up later. He was eager to talk, yet he felt that it would be better if Dad prompted the subject.

The restaurant was almost empty when they walked in. Even with the early hour, the hostess welcomed them with a bright smile. They asked if they could be seated at a large table. Besides the food, they needed extra space for their charts and magazines.

It did not take long for breakfast to be served. Steve was chewing his food while trying to share with Dad his new discoveries.

"It is not only about customer DNA and giving service to our customers," he said excitedly. "It is about the hairdresser and our poor service ratio compared to hers. What about Sharon's sofa and what about our cycles with their odd behavior? I wonder, Dad, if there's something wrong in our own business DNA, and I see these three clusters of unfolding knowledge and...."

Dad asked Steve to slow down, as he had a hard time understanding him. He could see how excited Steve was, and he decided to put aside his strict insistence of self-discipline and basic table manners on this particular occasion.

"Steve, I really would like to talk about everything, but please try to put some order to your thoughts. And by the way, what's the matter with Sharon's sofa?"

Dad's question made Steve stop eating. It was Amos's friendship with Dad that prevented Steve from revealing the whole story and its lessons. However, Dad's comment helped Steve to calm down, and redirect his thought process.

"I will tell you about the sofa later, and Dad you're probably right—I guess I'm overexcited. I've been dumping on you too many things at once. I have so much to go over with you, but first things first—tell me about your chart, the one you left on top of some magazines; which we also need to talk about".

"I'll get to it soon," Dad said. "I started yesterday with telling you about my life experience—not only with the workmanship aspect of service, but also in what really lies behind it. I think the way you put it into the customer DNA concept is a unique approach, taking intuition together with life experience—which we need to expand upon. But first I think there are a few other important things to go over, and one of them is finances."

Dad paused, glanced at his chart and then said, "A few days ago I got a phone call from Mr. George Stanley, our bank vice president, asking for an urgent meeting to discuss our ability to pay some of our debts. So I had to go over a lot of data. While working on the stack of papers I got from our accountant, I was thinking of other subjects that could be a good source of information to show our capability to recuperate. I looked around the office, searched in old files, and then I came across a few business magazines I kept from a while ago. At the time, I took an idea or two from each magazine, and I put them aside knowing I would get back to them one day when I had free time."

While speaking, Dad laid his magazines on the table. "Here is one about servicing tools. It contains important information and technical data which could be valuable. It ties in with these two other magazines talking about new equipment and new technologies. I think we need to acquire them sooner rather than later, to help us retain our high level of quality and workmanship. Another one is about some accounting principles that are very important to keep us profitable; and this magazine, Steve, is responsible for the ten-year chart you have seen on my—oops, sorry—*our* desk."

Captivity and Frustration

Channeling Sketch

Dad reorganized the magazines to form a precise rectangular stack and placed his chart on top. He looked around until his eyes locked on an imaginary spot in space, and he was silent for a moment or two. Steve could tell Dad's mind was somewhere else. Dad laid his hand on his chart, looked at Steve, and continued. "Sometimes things can take a surprise turn and this magazine was there at the right juncture—but not only on one occasion. It was as if when one cycle was just closing, a new one opened."

Dad paused, took a breath and said, "And now let me tell you how it all started. After a few years of establishing our business, we were doing alright. Our craftsmanship, quality, and reputation, eventually paid off. We got a good base of customers; we managed to pay our bills and made a little profit too. Even with the economy's ups and downs, we managed to sustain our business. Then I decided that we needed to do more to improve our bottom line.

"We embarked on an extensive sales campaign coupled with some new service offerings; we guaranteed faster deliveries and better quality than our competition. I knew we were taking the risk of incurring the burden of our campaign costs without necessarily getting the payback. The market didn't respond right away. However, persistence and patience were key factors. After a while, our efforts paid off. We began seeing a growing demand for our services, and not because the economy was booming. Some of it must have been at the expense of our competitors. Eventually, when our customers got comfortable with our improved performance, things were really picking up. Until we reached a crisis...."

As Dad was describing the situation, Steve could tell by his face and tone of voice, that it was as if he was reliving the past. Dad reached for his cup, took another sip of coffee, and carried on.

"As we were getting more and more service requests, we extended our working hours to keep up with the demand. We began experiencing a situation where a few customers' orders were slipping away. We weren't so inundated with customer orders that we couldn't keep up with the overall demand. However, it was a glitch here and a glitch there where we were running short in our ability to deliver on some of our promised dates. We took notice and worked really hard to close the gap, and I felt we had the situation back under control. Until one day, when I got a call from an angry customer.

"This customer was ready to pull his order out, really upset at our inability to meet his promised date," Dad said. "He was so frustrated that I had to use all of my charm, credibility, and past good performance, in order to get us a second chance. He said to me, 'I will accept the delay this time, as long as you personally guarantee the new date will not be moved again.' That was really a bad sign, Steve. I knew if I did not do something to rapidly resolve the situation, similar phone calls would follow, and that is the last thing you want to happen. Unfortunately, it didn't take long before we got a few more upset customers.

Dad sighed and then continued, "On the one hand, we had something everyone would want. The surge in our customer demand yielded increased sales and potential profits. On the other, we were faced with a day-to-day struggle to deliver our service on time. When you set a standard of one hundred percent satisfaction, even a few unhappy customers is too many."

As Dad was talking, his phone rang. Dad looked down at the number and said to Steve, "It's an important customer, I have to take this." While he spoke on the phone, Steve couldn't help himself from taking the customer side. Dad's story about the angry customer made him think about Amos. "Hadn't Sharon and I been through a similar situation when Amos was late in delivering her grandma's sofa?

"I wonder how our customers had felt about the whole situation Dad is describing. Were they giving Dad some leeway due to their longtime business relationship with him and his good reputation? Or, were they accepting lateness because they had no other choice, like we were with Amos?"

Steve had a hard time seeing Dad as a captor. But he could definitely now see how customers could have felt captive, while Dad wasn't even aware of it.

"Sharon and I felt like we were being held captive at Amos's hands," Steve thought. "There wasn't much we could have done. We needed the sofa on time for the house party, and the closer it got to the event, there was no indication he would be late. When Sharon realized the situation, it was already too late—nothing could be done. We couldn't just go there, cancel the order, grab the half-stripped sofa, and walk away hoping to find somebody else who could finish the job—although at the time that's what we wanted to do most. We were totally frustrated and couldn't do much, but to eventually get it late after the house party. I can imagine Dad's aggravated customer experiencing a similar situation to Sharon's."

As Steve was thinking of it, he started drawing an imaginary scene of him and Sharon running away, holding a half-stripped sofa, pieces of fabric and padding flying all around, and Amos chasing them, crying, "Hey, stop, please give me a second chance! Or at least pay for the new fabric I ordered...."

He looked at his artwork and smiled. "What a great way to channel your frustration—by drawing a caricature of a most annoying situation."

With the vivid view of Sharon and him not being able to break away and Dad's story, Steve's mind was back to their customers.

"In a situation like Dad is describing, how long does it take before they will be looking to go elsewhere," Steve wondered. "The phone call Dad received from an angry customer was the first visible sign for one who is close—maybe too close—to breaking away. And what happens with customers who do not give any sign, at least not immediately? Will the customer stay with you or start seeking other possibilities while you are not even aware of it? How much work has to be done in order to discover and recover a doubting customer—let alone one who went somewhere else?"

Steve's train of thought was cut off by Dad, who had just finished his call.

Relentless Search

7:00 a.m.

The restaurant which had been almost empty when they walked in, was now slowly filling with other customers. The increasing background noise did not disturb Dad. Now back to telling his story, he was so focused that he did not even notice Steve's sketch.

"One night after another long frustrating day, I went to my office ready for another long battle," Dad carried on. "Paperwork and mail had been piling up on my desk for at least a week. I guess it often happens when you have to chase customer orders and juggle priorities all week long. While I was getting rid of junk mail, my eyes caught a title on the cover of a magazine. I decided to read the magazine right away. Steve, the subject that really grabbed my attention was titled 'On Cycles and Bottlenecks'.

"I said to myself 'What perfect timing' and opened the magazine, located the article and started reading through. Right at the beginning I came across an interesting suggestion that really hit home. And let me show you Steve."

Dad moved his chart aside and picked up the magazine from the stack underneath—which he brought earlier when they went for breakfast. He searched for the article inside, glanced through a few pages and pointed at a sentence he long ago marked:

> *The first step you have to take in order to break your business boundaries is to ask yourself, what is your bottleneck?*

Dad gauged Steve's reaction and said, "It was an eye-opener then, and even more so now—which I will explain later with its connection to my ten-year chart."

He then continued with his story of when he had seen the magazine for the first time. "I brushed quickly through the rest of the article just to see that I wasn't missing anything important. I decided to take on the boundary-breaking idea. When you have too many problems to deal with, you better focus on the most important one.

"I then asked myself, what is my bottleneck? I couldn't come to any conclusion. What appeared to be a simple question quickly turned into a very challenging issue—and I couldn't just put it aside."

Dad paused. "Steve, anyone who has been around long enough can relate to a bottleneck—which is something that holds up progress or slows down the whole process. And when your back is pressed against the wall, like mine was, the awareness must turn into an immediate action.

"So I was ready to roll up my sleeves, and go on a quest to figure out what our bottleneck is—or maybe better said, the mysterious entity that was holding us back. I spent all night thinking, and my mind drifted in all directions. At first, I was thinking maybe our bottleneck was in the service stations area where we fix our customers' tools."

"What do you mean by that; couldn't the service stations just make enough?" Steve interrupted.

"Well, I wasn't sure if we had sufficient capacity," Dad replied.

"So did you end up finding them as your bottleneck, or was it something else?" asked Steve.

"It wasn't that simple," Dad replied. "Being a major resource, our service stations seemed to be the most logical place to start with," he explained. "So I was running through my head how we service our tools, and what could be blocking us from getting more done. We had qualified and loyal employees and all the necessary equipment to perform the job. Nothing was missing from that angle. We put in extra hours to comply with the demand, yet there were customers who didn't get their order on time. I couldn't pinpoint what was the real problem. The more time I spent looking at what appeared to be the obvious bottleneck, the less clear it became.

"I didn't know where to go next, until it crossed my mind that maybe I had overlooked something in our customer demand. You know, Steve, we have many customers and give various types of service. Each order requires special attention, along with its own process and time to make it."

"Are you saying that the problem was not in the service stations but rather in our customers?" Steve asked. "That does not make any sense."

"No no," Dad laughed. "What I mean is that sometimes your customers want a certain type of service more than the other. Consequently, it can cause a shift in workload and create a bottleneck—which eventually hurts your ability to deliver service on time."

"Can you clarify it?" Steve inquired.

"Let's use again our hairdresser example," Dad replied. "Imagine that suddenly all of her customers would be asking for styling and coloring, instead of regular hairstyling. What would happen to her capacity?"

"Well, I think it would...." Steve said, but Dad didn't let him finish.

"You see Steve, since styling and coloring take at least twice as much time as just regular hairstyling, I bet you she would only be able to serve at about half of her normal capability—thus becoming a bottleneck. Isn't it true?"

Without letting Steve respond he continued, "What makes it even more confusing, is that she might not even realize she had a bottleneck. Her daily revenue stream may not even change—for probably charging double for coloring and styling. Yet, she will have to push too many customers out while not internalizing the magnitude of the problem."

Dad paused. "Then what would happen all the while with these customers, and how long would they be willing to wait before they became upset?"

He looked at Steve, waiting for his reply.

"I think I got it," Steve answered. "The hairdresser is in fact no different from one of our service stations. The type of work she does for each customer and the time it takes, determines how many customers she can serve in a day. And even if the flow of incoming orders remains the same, requesting a different type of service may create—out of nowhere—a block in the ability to serve everyone."

And then he added, "Couldn't the same logic apply to us and to anyone who performs any type of service?"

"You are absolutely right," Dad said. "Perhaps we saw customer orders coming in at a normal rate, but we didn't fully realize the amount of special work they required—by then it was already too late."

"So in the end, did you manage to identify the problem?" Steve asked.

Dad took a long breath. "I did not stop there. I looked deeper into our service stations process. Was it in an employee with exceptional skills—thereby excess work was unintentionally channeled toward him? Maybe it was in a piece of equipment that did not function well? Did we unnoticeably shift our skilled resources to deal with oddball orders?

"Then I looked even further. I was trying to see if there were other areas or aspects that could be our bottleneck. Was it in the way we received and processed our orders? Was it because we became careless and jumped on every opportunity—which may not have been best suited to our capabilities? Perhaps it was it in the way we scheduled the work, or simply that we promised a service response time we couldn't meet?

"I couldn't come to any conclusion," Dad said. "My mind was getting dizzy trying to figure out what our bottleneck is and where it might be. It was getting late and everything looked scrambled. Yet, I wasn't ready to give up."

Intangible Reality

Dad was interrupted by the waitress, who came to offer a fresh coffee refill. He asked for some more, but Steve decided to pass. As their attention had shifted momentarily from Dad's story, Steve realized that he had not called Sharon yet. It was too late to call her the night before, but Steve felt it would be inexcusable not to call her soon. The timing was just right, and he asked Dad to take a few minutes' break.

"I can use a short break too," Dad said, and both of them left the table.

Steve called Sharon. He didn't need to explain not calling and staying at work all night, as Sharon completely understood the situation. After all she had offered her full support. He briefed her on what had happened since they had last spoken. There was a lot to cover, but he focused on Dad's chart and his story of relentless bottleneck search. He did not mention the phone call from Mr. Bupti.

After listening to Steve, she said, "Darling, you have been through a lot in one night, and I'm sure you and Dad have much to discuss. Whatever it is, I hope you find the answers. With the little sleep you have had, please do not overstress yourself." She sent her love and wished him a productive morning.

Steve went back to their table, but Dad was not there yet. He reread the marked sentence in the magazine. Breaking boundaries and Dad's story of his efforts to figure out what was holding them back, provoked a thought. "Maybe, as Dad said, the bottleneck was not in the service stations area? Maybe it lies somewhere else, in places which are not as obvious?

"Dad looked at the change in customers' demand as another possibility," Steve thought. "But it is intangible. How do you get a hold of it? In what way do you quantify it? How could it become a bottleneck, and what do you do to resolve it?"

With these questions in mind he tried to go through the other possible bottleneck areas, and see which elements were obvious and which were not.

On a piece of paper he wrote the possibilities Dad mentioned, in his quest of finding the limiting factor. Next to each one he noted:

Bottlenecks ???

Service Stations   — Physical - Tangible

Workers   — Physical - Tangible

Tools & Equipment   — Physical - Tangible

Unique Skills   - Abstract - Intangible

Customer Orders & Mix Change - Abstract - Intangible

Work Scheduling   - Abstract - Intangible

Response Time & Delivery - Abstract - Intangible

Looking at his list he thought, "There are at least as many intangible elements as tangible ones. I bet if one looks deeper, a few more will pop up. Is it possible that the benefits of resolving intangible bottlenecks are greater than fixing the *obvious* tangible ones?"

To put things in a better order he decided to use the same charting technique, as he had when analyzing Amos's flow of events in the sofa saga. "Dad's story described a stressful situation as well. So looking at the overall process with its service cycle could help here too."

Steve then drew their process chart. He sketched Dad's customers placing orders, tools piling up in front of the service centers—while their loyal employees work hard, trying to catch up with the demand; and the search for bottlenecks along the entire service cycle.

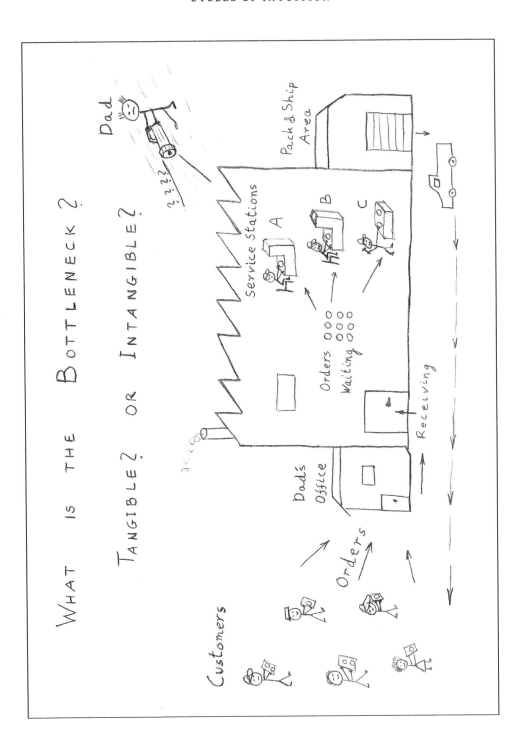

"Some more art, sketches, and caricatures—I'm really getting better at it," Steve thought smiling. "Maybe it's about time to show Sharon this new side of me."

Before getting too cocky he put his sketch away with the rest of his charts, and he was back to his list of possible bottlenecks. "It's a whole different reality. I wonder how many people are even aware of intangible bottlenecks. I bet most would focus on the tangible ones. Is that why, all too often, people get frustrated as their efforts yield little, if any, bottom line results?"

Traffic Jam and Illusive Bottlenecks

Dad was back a couple of minutes after Steve finished his chart. He sat on his chair. "So Steve, where did I leave off with my story? By the way, did you manage to get Sharon? I'm sorry it took me a bit long. I was talking to Mom. I told her you were at the office all night, and that we had continued discussing important issues at Jim's place—but at least now we are enjoying a good breakfast together."

"I talked to Sharon, and I told her about your bottleneck search," Steve answered. "There is where you left off." He was tempted to tell Dad about the intangible bottleneck idea, but he didn't want to divert the conversation, as he was eager to hear the rest of the story.

"Anyway, I was struggling that night to find out what was holding us back," Dad continued. "It was getting late, and eventually I decided to go home. I thought that a break and rest would help me refocus. But there were so many unanswered questions that I couldn't sleep all night. So I concluded that instead of struggling alone, I would do it with a group."

He paused. "Son, when you pinpoint the problem, it is almost like finding the entire solution. Having that in focus can propel a stream of great ideas.

Then, you can take corrective actions and get back on track. You can do it yourself or even better—bring other people in for the task. You will be surprised what a group of people can do, when geared toward a specific target. And if the target is a bottleneck, then creativity, ideas and solutions will follow. That's exactly what I decided to do."

"I think it is an excellent idea," Steve interjected, cutting Dad's story off. "But what can you do if all you have is you? Who are you going to consult with?" Steve asked.

Dad stopped. "What makes you ask this question, son?"

"A few days ago Sharon shared with me that she would like to open her own business and use her arts skills for something besides teaching," Steve replied.

"Is that so? Dad responded. "It seems that the entrepreneurial spirit runs in the family. I congratulate Sharon for her initiative; please pass it along." He then continued, "Well, Steve, to instinctively answer your question, Sharon has you to consult with. I will also be happy to assist once she is in real need."

He took a pause. "I believe that if any person simply opens his mind, they can always find someone to consult with—whether it's a friend, a family member, or anybody who has been through a similar experience."

He then smiled, "It seems the two of you are going to be very busy in the near future. Not only will you be able to give her advice here and there, but she will probably be able to help you too. Now that we have solved that, can we continue?"

"So I decided to gather our people first thing in the morning, present them with the situation, ask them the questions I have asked myself, and get their perspective. Then, my plan was to get all of us on the same path, hopefully to find what our bottleneck is. From there, figure out what to do in order to improve our capabilities and hopefully get back on track with our customers."

Dad stopped and asked rhetorically, "After all, isn't it about satisfying our customers and making some money too?"

Without allowing Steve to reply he carried on. "In the morning I was driving to work, and my mind was running twice as fast as my car. All of a sudden, I had to slam on the brakes. I guess when your mind is overly occupied you lose concentration. I probably didn't keep enough distance from the car in front, which had stopped abruptly. Somehow I managed to avoid the collision, and my car stopped just a mere inch from the other vehicle. We stalled for a few seconds, allowing me to recuperate. Then traffic began moving and it did not take long before we stopped again.

"For the next few minutes we would accelerate. Then all of a sudden we'd stop, reaccelerate, stop again...and eventually we came to a complete halt. It was not clear what was going on. Had there been a car accident, road construction ahead, or maybe a car had broken down, blocking traffic? But one thing was for sure. I was stuck in a traffic jam and in front of me was a long line of cars—all held back by an unknown cause for the bottleneck. While sitting in the car, it crossed my mind that our business's situation was similar to the traffic jam I was in. The only difference was, however, I knew that eventually I would get out of the traffic gridlock. But I was not sure if I would get out of our business one.

"When I finally got to the shop, I gathered our people for an emergency meeting and presented them with the facts—at least the way I saw our situation. Steve, I could probably write a book about what had transpired, but instead I'll give you a quick summary."

Dad took a sip of his coffee. "It's getting cold," he mumbled and carried on. "We discussed at length what was going on in almost every aspect of our business: what happens with our customer orders, how late they are, and the problems from each person's perspective. It felt as if we had been going in circles. We found ourselves agreeing on a subject and then not long after going back to debating the same one. Each one of us had many ideas and suggestions for corrective actions. I guess they all had to do with important issues, but it was as though we were lacking focus.

"As we continued our analysis, it seemed that our bottleneck was becoming even more elusive. In fact, it felt as though there wasn't a single area that did not seem to be a holdup—in one way or another. Finally, we got back on track. We decided to list our problems and organize them in a descending order. We put on the top of the list those with the heaviest weight and at the bottom the lightest. From there we went on to associate the top listed with their assumed causes."

Dad's description of prioritizing the problems, reminded Steve again of the Pareto principle—of focusing on the important few elements which affect the most. It was similar to his approach of dealing with their top three customers, in his action list of implementing customer DNA.

Dad continued. "To make a long story short, we came up with two key items that we all agreed were our main bottlenecks. One was our service capacity for certain tools. Only one person was an expert in fixing them, and it was where we saw a shift in our customer demand. The other was the way we were quoting delivery for our customers. The service time we were promising was too short compared to reality, further aggravating the situation. So the course of action was to expand our capacity in the service area—by training another worker to be able to service special tools as well. We also began quoting realistic service times, which would reflect the dynamics of our business and our ability to deliver."

Dad paused. There was a hint of a smile on his face, as if he was satisfied for finally finding a solution to a complex problem.

He then said, "We were successful in both of our bottleneck areas. In a relatively short time, we had managed to improve things. We increased our service abilities, and scheduled our work in a priority manner. An order with the longest delay to the customer's requested date was serviced first. Then we serviced the next one, working our way through the entire list of late orders.

"We had a higher rate of sales, and our late orders list was getting smaller. I was very satisfied with our progress, and I felt that by focusing on our key issues, we turned the situation around and our bottom line reflected that."

"So what happened then?" Steve asked.

Dad took a long breath and said, "Then out of nowhere the bottom fell out."

Keep for Review at a Later Date

There was a moment of silence and then Steve said, "How could that be?"

"Well, Steve, I am not really sure," Dad replied. He shook his head as though he was attempting to come back from his journey in time.

He then continued. "As I told you we were enjoying a few months of success while catching up with our customer orders. Then all of a sudden the demand fell off and our entire situation turned south, as well as our bottom line. The shop was almost empty and consequently our bottlenecks disappeared."

Steve was astounded by the sudden turn in the story. "Was there a downturn in the economy which caused an abrupt recession?"

"No, the overall economy was stable at that time," Dad responded.

"Is it possible then, that there was a problem in our specific market segment?" Steve continued.

"I thought it was," Dad answered, "but when I checked what was happening with our competition, they were doing well—in fact maybe too well, probably at our expense."

Steve couldn't comprehend Dad's explanation. "But Dad, you were doing the right things. What went wrong?"

"I don't exactly know," Dad said with a sigh. "At the time I could only speculate. But more importantly I had to get some business back in a hurry. We were scratching for work, and instead of putting my energy to things I really love, I was back on the selling job. Rather than finding better ways to improve our technical abilities and helping our people hone their skills, I found myself calling customers all day long. This time however, not to apologize for pushing delivery dates out. Instead, I was trying to attract business by offering customers quicker delivery and even some upfront discounts."

Even though the events took place a long time ago, Steve could tell by Dad's expression that he was still troubled as though it had happened recently.

"I couldn't afford to spend time analyzing what might have gone wrong," Dad continued. "The wheel had turned upside down, and our notion of resolving bottlenecks had evaporated almost overnight. Imagine Steve, how I felt when one of our employees was asking where our workload had suddenly disappeared to. He and the other guys had put a lot of hard work into the bottlenecks undertaking. I wasn't sure whether he was cynical or simply expressing his frustration and fear for the future. As their lead man I didn't have any good answers to give, except to stick to our guns and continue servicing at the highest quality while pursuing more sales. Eventually we succeeded. I had to work really hard to slowly bring our customers back. I struggled with day-to-day issues in order to provide a good service and re-stabilize our situation."

Dad sighed and then pointed at the open magazine lying on the corner of their breakfast table. The faded color of the marked sentence regarding bottleneck and breaking boundaries, reflected the passage of time. "With the change of circumstances, I couldn't find its relevance anymore. I filed it with a note saying 'Keep for review at a later date,' and so it lay there with the other magazines for a long time."

Rise and Fall of the Momentum Wheel

8:00 am

The restaurant was getting quieter as people were finishing breakfast and rushing to work. Still, there were a few more customers beside Dad and Steve. The waiters were clearing leftover food and plates from the tables. Dad and Steve were so deep in thought that they didn't notice what was going on around them. Dad's story, with its unexpected end, left each wondering what might have gone wrong.

When the waitress came to check on them, Steve realized that with their intense discussion, he had left half of his food on the plate. Even the coffee had gotten cold. Dad, being so occupied telling his story, had barely touched his food as well.

Coming back to the present, Dad said, "A few years have passed and things have taken a surprising turn—sometimes a crisis can give birth to new opportunities."

He paused. "As you recall, Steve, a few days ago Mr. Stanley had called for an urgent meeting at the bank. I spent hours in compiling information. I worked hard, thinking of how to present our ability to recover and meet our financial obligations. As I was preparing the material, I came across the old magazines—those I file for review at a later time. I looked at each of them again, and with the view of our current situation I put aside the few that seemed most relevant to our recovery plan."

Dad pointed at his stack of articles and said, "Steve, they are all important, but re-discovering the article about cycles and bottlenecks was as if I was struck by lightning. I realized that back then, in my quest for resolving our situation, I was probably over-simplifying the whole notion that it was intending to bring. I was only looking at one side of the coin, the bottleneck aspect, without taking into account the other side—the changing behavior over time."

"Behavior of what?" Steve interjected, trying to comprehend Dad's words.

"Behavior of cycles," Dad replied.

He searched for his marker pen. Dad used to carry it along, to always be prepared for highlighting important information—on drawings, documents, books, and magazines.

He then marked a sentence next to the old one and read it aloud:

The first step you have to take in order to break your business boundaries is to ask yourself, what is your bottleneck?

And you have to do it while understanding cycles over time.

Dad tapped the page and said, "It became clear to me that I had to look at the two sentences of the paragraph together, rather than focusing on the first one alone. Perhaps with the passage of time you can get a whole new perspective."

"How would you connect between the two?" Steve asked.

"Well, I did the first step by taking the cycles notion and preparing our past ten years sales chart," Dad answered. "As to the next step—of linking it all together—that is exactly what I intend to figure out with your help, son."

He then continued, "If I have to judge by my actions back then, it seems as though I had started well. But, I don't think that at the time I had fully understood the root cause of the situation we were in. First, out of nowhere we had a growing number of angry customers, frustrated with late deliveries. Then after taking corrective actions, we were catching up. Our customers appeared to be happier with our service, and we made some money too. While everything seemed to be stabilizing, the bottom suddenly fell out. Maybe with the first sign of an upset customer we were already in big trouble."

Dad sighed. "The momentum of the wheel was too strong."

"What do you mean by momentum and what wheel, Dad?"

Dad took a minute and replied, "Maybe when you are under the gun you tend to rush things and take shortcuts, or perhaps the success of overcoming the crisis blinded me. I guess that when I had been busy in my bottleneck search and the evolving efforts to fix our situation, I might have lost some of my sensitivity to our customers' satisfaction. So, while I was convinced I was getting the situation under control, some of them might have decided to place their future orders with competitors. As we were catching up, we might not have realized that our customer base was eroding. The momentum of losing customers was probably already ahead of us, and we were not seeing it at all. By the time we saw it, the bottom fell out and it was already too late. You see Steve, you can use the momentum wheel as an analogy for what is coming your way from all of your customers. And we were seeing the back of it instead. If you see it from the front, you can tell ahead of time when the demand is on the rise or when it begins to head south. At least it is my analogy for how things work."

As Dad was talking passionately about understanding what might have gone wrong, Steve thought to himself, "So we do have *bye* customers as well. That's exactly what Dad is describing and apparently it all happened without an early warning sign—at least not one that he noticed."

Going along with Dad's analogy, Steve could picture a huge wheel rolling uphill, representing customers' orders piling up—a desired situation of increasing demand and sales.

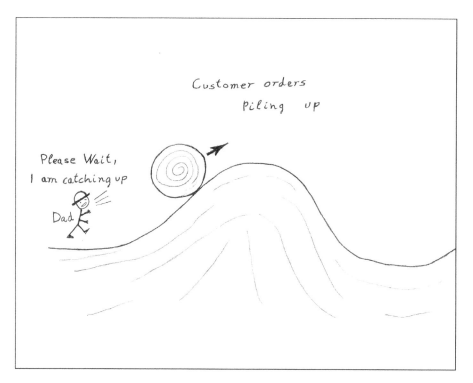

Suddenly the wheel started rolling downhill with increasing speed, as a symbol of a sharp decline. And all the while Dad was chasing the wheel from behind, with *bye* customers jumping off the wheel in its sharp descent.

With the view of the customers' momentum wheel Steve asked, "Are you suggesting, Dad, that all of your effort resolving bottlenecks and late delivery improvement was done for nothing?"

"I still would have done the same thing, and I know it was all valuable," Dad replied. "Had we not done it, our situation would have been even worse. However, in retrospect, I think that with a better understanding, we could have avoided major stress when demand was on the rise. And even better, we could have avoided the fall."

Steve had many questions to ask but he asked only one: "That is a very strong statement, Dad. But what was missing then?"

Unpredictability in a Predictable Pattern

For a moment Dad was silent. He scratched his head while trying to answer Steve. "I'm not really sure... that is exactly what we need to find. We have to develop the ability to see the momentum wheel turning ahead, instead of seeing it from behind."

The grandfather clock by the far end of the wall caught Steve's attention. It was a genuine antique kept in mint condition—handed down to Jim, the restaurant owner, by his grandfather. The pendulum swung from side to side in perfect rhythm. The view of the pendulum in motion triggered an idea in Steve's mind. He pointed at it and said "Dad, look at the pendulum's motion."

The sudden diversion of their conversation took Dad by surprise. "I see it, but what do you have in mind?"

"Maybe the pendulum motion and the rolling wheel going up and down the hill are not much different from each other," Steve replied. "I have a hunch it is connected to cycles and the ticking of time—which could unveil the pattern of our ups and downs."

Dad couldn't comprehend. "I see the pendulum and I can envision the rolling wheel. But what is the connection, and how does it tie in with our situation?"

"It will become clear in a moment," Steve answered, "On my morning walk I was thinking of your ten-year chart you left on our office table—with its pattern like a mountain skyline. Yet it looks as if it has some repeatability in its ups and downs. So I was trying to see if its pattern has anything to do with seasonality."

He presented his seasonality chart and pointed at the transitions from one season to another.

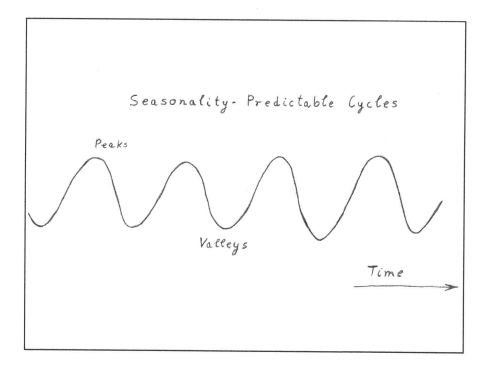

Steve then continued. "You see, Dad, the pendulum has a perfectly steady cycle. It moves in a predictable order—so are the cycles when dealing with seasonality. We can draw a parallel between the two. The peaks and valleys are repetitive and they come over and over again like the motion of the grandfather clock's pendulum. However, their frequency is different. Seasonality changes every few months and the pendulum by seconds. So in essence both patterns represent a steady change—from high to low in seasonality, and from side to side in the pendulum motion."

He let Dad absorb the thought and then added, "Maybe we also have a repetitive pattern of a different frequency for our business ups and downs— for whatever cause."

Dad was trying to figure out Steve's idea and asked, "Even if it is the case, what would you do about it?"

"With seasonality, the cycles are predictable and the fashion business is a good example," Steve replied. "There, they probably develop a plan based on past behavior of their cycles and adjust accordingly. So we can do the same. In fact if I understand the article suggestions about cycles and bottlenecks interconnectivity, we have it all here"

Steve had a big grin on his face. For a moment he felt like he was in front of his class in college, presenting a bright solution for a complex problem.

"Making a plan based on cycles sounds like an excellent idea," Dad said. "But even with seasonality, how would the plan hold?"

"It will hold because of its predictable pattern," Steve insisted.

Maybe I'm too old, or you are simply running too fast with your thoughts," Dad said, not wanting to downplay Steve's enthusiasm. "But unless I don't understand your seasonality chart, I see unpredictability in its predictable pattern."

Steve was puzzled. "What do mean by unpredictability in seasonality, Dad? It sounds like a contradiction."

"Well, I can definitely see how the cycles are predictable by the virtue of seasonality" Dad said. "And they do come back again and again. That is exactly what your chart shows. But not everything is repeatable."

He stood up and pointed dramatically at the grandfather clock. "Unlike the pendulum's precise side-to-side motion, the peaks on your chart don't have the same height and the valleys don't share the same depth, and that's what happens in real life."

He then continued. "Steve, unless your hand was shaky because of early morning low blood sugar, I assume your chart intended to show just that."

Steve took a minute to digest Dad's point of view and said, "I cannot guarantee my hand wasn't shaky, but you are right. I did not intend that the peaks and valleys be the same from season to season."

"So you see, Steve, that's exactly what I meant when I said I see unpredictability in the predictable cycles. In general their timing is predictable, but their magnitude is not. It's like anticipating a wave. You know it will arrive but you don't know its size in advance, and that is a major problem we need yet to overcome."

Wave Surfing and Hawaiian Punch

The restaurant was almost empty, and Dad standing up while giving his explanation and pointing at the grandfather clock, had grabbed not only Steve's attention. The waiters, who were organizing things around, stopped their work for a minute as well.

Dad continued. "To sum things up; unlike the pendulum, seasonality cycles have unpredictable magnitude, which means you have to guess what's coming your way. I don't have experience in running a clothing store, but when it comes to unpredictable magnitudes, I have seen it all."

Dad, who was still standing, realized that the waiters had stopped working, as they were watching him. Embarrassed, he nodded his head with an apology for taking center stage. He sat, toned down his voice and continued his explanation.

"Steve, if I take your example of the fashion business, then as a customer, you see seasonality only through the items you buy—summer or winter clothes. But as a service provider, you see it in a totally different way. Every new season you have to stock new goods, put old ones on sale, move things around, change displays, manage your inventory, reorganize everything, and what not."

"And I believe it may get even more complicated than that," Dad mumbled, and then continued by posing a question. "Are you able to know in advance the exact change in your demand for a specific season? Imagine that by using past experience, you plan to increase your resources and inventory by twenty percent in anticipation for the upcoming season. But what would happen if the actual upswing is forty percent instead? Wouldn't you have, all of a sudden, a major bottleneck?"

Listening to Dad, Steve was quiet. After all, he had a lot of good old-time values and manners, being raised in a small Midwest town.

Dad paused while trying to read Steve's expression and then said, "Let's continue with the bottleneck situation. With the forty percent increase, you don't have enough merchandise on display, and your warehouse is emptying out faster than you plan. Your suppliers adjusted their deliveries based on your schedule for twenty percent increase. But, they as well, can't instantly match to the actual forty percent grow in demand. And on top of everything, you have too many customers who don't get what they want.

"Your entire workforce is stressed out, you lose potential sales, and the whole chain is falling apart. It is a ripple effect, where the pressure extends down the chain. So Steve, do we have here a problem or not?"

Dad was on a roll with his explanation. This time, however, he was talking about the other side of unpredictability.

"We did not discuss yet what happens when you plan for a twenty percent upswing, and you get no actual increase at all. You have your staff and merchandise in place. But the expected customers' demand is not there. What do you do then?"

Steve was silent, processing Dad's argument in his mind. He then said, "I guess you are right. Even if you have seasonality, the unpredictable magnitude of a swing can make the model fall apart. You really don't know what's coming ahead. Is it going to be a bottleneck situation or insufficient workload instead? Is it going to be a surging wave of demand where you barely keep your head above water, or is it a shallow one hardly challenging your capabilities?"

Steve paused, and in his mind he pictured a wave watching scene in Hawaii. A crowd of surfers was chasing unpredictable waves; they were all competing who will win—riding the highest one. All the while he and Dad were relaxing nearby on their beach chairs, sipping fruit-punch cocktails—betting on who will fall and who will win?

Steve's imaginary scene of wave surfing competition was brought to an end by Dad making a surprising statement. "You see son, even though there are disturbing shortfalls in using seasonality as a model, there are some merits in exploring it."

He put the charts next to each other and said, "Our ten-year chart pattern looks different than your seasonality one. But your observation, that we may have repeatability in our ups and downs, cannot be ignored."

Dad pointed at his chart:

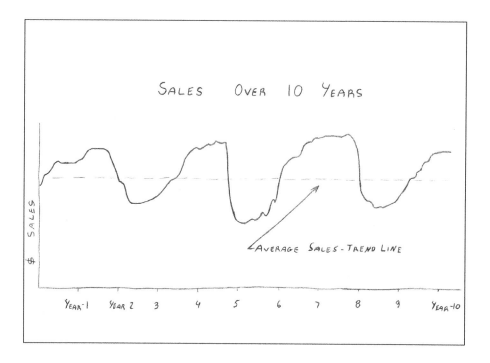

He then tapped the page, "Steve, we are going to put our minds together. Although it is very important to start with challenging yourself to find your bottleneck, it must be linked to the evolving cycles over time. We must understand our cycles and have to find the answer today. We are not leaving until we do."

He looked at his weary son and said, "I know how tired you must be. Why don't we refill our cups?" He signaled the waitress. Within a few minutes, she was back with clean cups and fresh coffee.

Dad continued, pointing at the chart's sharp peaks and valleys. "The phone call from Mr. Stanley inadvertently made me reread the article and it was responsible for making this chart. So this time, I feel we are at a juncture where we have an opportunity to change things around. Not only show the bank our ability to meet our financial obligations, but break our own boundaries for the long haul.

"I guess two heads working together are better than one. Your knowledge from college may be helpful in figuring out the charts, as I do find them fairly complex."

As Dad was going through his explanation, Steve could feel how the article was shaping into something new. Not only with the content it was suggesting, but with a new role—a guide in their journey. He could not see in it a "Do this or that" like a recipe in a cook book. Rather, it was more suggestive in giving hints and insights to be further explored.

A Blindfolded Intuition

Dad's phone rang. Mr. George Stanley's secretary was on the line. "Can you please hold on for a moment," Dad said. He covered the phone and said in an aside to Steve, "Maybe it is sooner than I anticipated," and he was back to the call.

The phone call was short. "I would like to schedule a meeting with Mr. Stanley for tomorrow afternoon," She said. Dad asked for more time so they could come better prepared.

"Let me check with Mr. Stanley and I'll get back to you," She said, ending the call.

Dad looked at Steve and said, "Well, my intuition regarding the upcoming meeting wasn't that far off. We have to come up with a strategy and show our plan—demonstrating our ability to pay."

For a moment they looked at each other, not sure how to proceed—as if the phone call had broken their train of thought. Then Dad said, "Our current situation is better than it was, and our customer demand is on the rise. If we can understand how to retain it and avoid the next fall, we will be able, soon enough, to reduce our debts. That is what we have to show our bank."

He then continued. "Steve, with your attempt to compare our situation to cycles of seasonality, we might have stepped on something. I think it lies with comprehending unpredictability, and from there developing a method to overcome its downward spiraling effects."

Dad then smiled and said, "I told you that your understanding of charts can lead the way."

"Thanks Dad, but how do we implement that idea?" Steve replied, somewhat embarrassed.

"I'm not exactly sure, Steve," Dad responded. "But thinking about what we discussed so far, maybe our strategy should be based on three steps: First, understanding the cycles, second planning ahead, and third, adjusting capabilities accordingly"

Dad paused. "However, to be candid, I'm not sure how to put it into practice."

They both were quiet for a short while, and then Steve said, "So if you have the right approach but you don't have the solution, how do you carry forward?"

Dad hesitated and then said, "I guess you have to rely on your intuition."

"Would that be sufficient?" Steve asked.

"There is nothing wrong with it and you should use your intuition as much as you can," Dad replied. "But when things get complicated it may not be enough—especially when you have cycles and unpredictable situations."

Steve looked at Dad and tried to comprehend his notion. He then said, "Dad, with knowing so many friends and with your years of experience, is running the business by intuition unique to a very few—or is it common for many?"

"Thinking about it, I'm afraid that too many belong to the 'running by intuition' category." Dad replied. "I guess as long as things are stable and predictable, intuitive decisions are probably sufficient and effective. But such situations are very rare. Using my experience, stability only holds for a short time. It gives you a false sense of certainty. But after a while, you realize things shift around at random and then you begin to fall behind."

He then pointed at Steve's seasonality chart and said, "At first it looked simple. But our analysis of seasonality reveals so much uncertainty within assumed stability, that I cannot even imagine what happens in more complex situations."

Taking Dad's words in, Steve summarized, "It seems that there are very few, if any, situations of stability in real life. I'm not sure how many people are even aware of cycles, their unpredictable magnitude, and the compound effect they bring.

"So managing by intuition in volatile cycles, is like a ship's captain being blindfolded, sailing his small boat in the middle of a stormy ocean. Feeling the rough wave motion, he is singing happily with the help of a drink or two—trying his best to steer it to the haven of secure anchorage."

He then continued. "Look at us Dad, aren't we in the same boat? How many years of experience are required before you become a craftsman in your trade? And how many years pass before you start asking questions about your business behavior over time, and its cycles? Where do you gain such knowledge?

"I am not sure, Steve," Dad replied. "But keep doing 'more of the same' will not get you that far. Maybe facing a crisis can propel unexpected solutions and help you leap beyond intuition—especially if you keep your mind open."

Dad took a minute and said, "I think just putting the cycles chart in front of anybody, as we had, is like taking off the blindfold from the boat captain's eyes. All of a sudden, you see the reality of the waves and you can decide what to do—ignore them or start taking control."

He then continued. "We just began looking into cycles, and at the moment I feel our boat is very small and the waves are too high. Steve, we don't have the option of your captain removing the blindfold, and at the frightening sight of the stormy seas he instantly puts it back on—taking another drink and holding the steering wheel very tightly. The more we become aware of waves and their impact, the less we have the luxury of closing our eyes."

Dad's explanation was interrupted by the ring of his phone. Mr. Stanley's secretary was calling in.

Conflict of Interpretations

9:30 a.m.

"I checked with Mr. Stanley," she told Dad. "Unfortunately he will be tied up after tomorrow, and it might be for a while. He has some urgent things to deal with, and is also expecting a guest from overseas. So your meeting must remain for tomorrow afternoon. He asked that you bring over whatever material you have, even if it's not fully prepared."

"It is a done deal then," Dad replied. "We will do our best to be fully prepared."

"We will see you tomorrow," she said, and wished him a good day.

Dad pulled out his pocket calendar, marked the appointment, and told Steve about what she had to say.

It was simply the right timing, and the mentioning of Mr. Stanley guest from overseas, that prompted Steve to tell Dad about Mr. Bupti.

"Dad, I had this strange call in the middle of night," and he went on to tell Dad the whole story.

He took a breath and then said, "And what bothers me most is Mr. Bupti's mentioning of rumors about our financial difficulties. How in the world did he get this information, and what made him ask if we are up for sale? I have no idea who he is, except being from far away and his distinct accent. Could he be the guest from overseas Mr. Stanley is waiting to see?"

Steve stopped right there. He felt he might have gone too far. "Dad, maybe I am getting too paranoid, but my intuition is telling that there is something behind all this."

He hesitated. "Tell me Dad, are we really up for sale?"

Although Dad was entirely taken aback by Steve's story, he felt he needed to stop it from sliding too far. "No, Steve, we are not up for sale. I would have told you that right from the start. Maybe it is simply your interpretation from the rapid turn of events."

Dad took a minute. "Sometimes you can get a biased reading from random occurrences. Maybe, as he said, Mr. Bupti got his information from his relatives, and possibly set his eyes on our service enterprise for quite sometime. Being smart to sense an opportunity and with the economy recent slowdown, he could have just made a wise guess."

He looked at Steve and added, "Yet, there is something I am bothered by. In order to relieve the pressure, I talked confidentially with some very close friends and asked if they could help. I was hoping we can get some financial aid, pay the bank, and get it off our back."

Dad smiled. "I know how to deal better with friends; and by the way you know one of them very well."

"Who is he?" Steve asked.

"Amos," Dad replied. "I trust his integrity and that of my other friends. Yet nowadays of advanced communication, some information might have leaked out. Anyway, Steve, would that be a reason to deter us from moving forward?

"I am sure it won't," Dad rhetorically said. "And regarding Mr. Bupti's meeting Mr. Stanley at the bank, we will eventually find out."

Dad signaled the waitress and the unfinished breakfast was cleared off the table. The open table space allowed Dad to put their charts in the center.

"So how do you suggest continuing on with the journey?" Steve asked.

"At the moment it's like we are holding a flashlight," Dad replied. "It doesn't give you the full view, but it shows you the way in the dark. We have our charts, we have the awareness, and we have the passion to find a better way. So, as we move along we really have to understand our cycles without taking shortcuts. We already discussed what could happen in the fashion business. But to get a better understanding, I suggest we look together at different examples as well."

Steve was ready to suggest Amos. He had already done a lot of thinking while he was trying to figure out customer DNA and service ratio. However he decided not to recommend Amos, as he was not sure Dad would be able to maintain objectivity hearing about his poor service regarding Sharon's sofa. Instead, he suggested their imaginary hairdresser.

"I like the idea of bringing her back" Dad said. "Not to discuss how her service cycle works for a single customer. That we already covered in depth. This time however, we need to find what the demand pattern is—for all of her customers."

Carrying the idea further Dad said humorously, "Imagine she is sitting with us over our long breakfast and participating in our brainstorming discussion. I'm sure she would love Jim's breakfast, as he is the best in town, and I hope we would be considered good company."

With the imaginary scenario in mind Dad added, "So how about we first ask our hairdresser to draw her chart over a few years? Of course we have to make clear the exact information she has to gather. Which type of data would you suggest, Steve?"

"I would look at her sales figures over time—the same way you made your chart, Dad. Since collecting the information may take too long, why don't we ask her to look at her monthly revenues over the past two years? From there, we may be able to see if she has seasonality or any other cyclical pattern."

And then Steve stopped. "I guess we are stuck. If we want to continue our simulation, we need to have a real hairdresser sitting with us. Otherwise, we have no tangible information to make anything conclusive."

Steve was silent for a moment. He looked at Dad and then at the chair next to their table, unoccupied by the imaginary hairdresser. He sighed. "I wish she would actually be sitting here with us. Instead of theorizing and toying with possibilities, we then could simply ask her how her business works. Maybe she would be giving us different insights."

"You are full of surprises, Steve." Dad said. "You just gave me an idea. I think Janet has a day off, so why don't I give her a call and ask her to join us for breakfast?"

Dad stood up and said, "We were so preoccupied before, that we didn't eat much. I believe that both of us will be more than satisfied with a second round. Please excuse me for a minute."

And off he went to make his telephone call.

Second Breakfast with Janet

Twenty minutes later, Janet walked in and joined them.

Janet and Dad first met at a chamber of commerce conference and had become close friends in the many years since. Her quick mind and witty tongue never ceased to amaze Dad. She was well-respected among all the members as a very smart business person. She opened her hair salon, which, years later, expanded to become the only beauty salon in town. It had two sections, one for hair care and another for beauty treatments. There were other salons in town, but she was the only one that offered hair and beauty treatments in one place. She ran the hair care section of the business, while her daughter Caroline took care of the beauty treatments.

"So gentlemen, to whom do I owe the honor to be invited for an unusual breakfast at twenty minutes notice?" Janet asked, with a smile lighting up her face—matching her stylish appearance as a beauty salon owner.

"Cycles," Dad and Steve answered simultaneously.

That was the last thing Janet expected to hear. "I was convinced that you were going to tell me about an upcoming celebration for Steve and Sharon finally tying the knot. After such a nice open house party, I expected it to be their next big event!"

"That may be coming sometime in the future," Dad replied while looking at Steve with a hint of a smile. "But we are here to discuss other matters."

It took more than a few minutes for Dad to cover the whole story of his plans to turn over the business to Steve. "My decision gave me the opportunity to look back and re-evaluate my life's endeavor—as well as the shortfalls along the way.

"You see Janet, now I understand that while providing our service I was caught in a trap. Dealing with one crisis after another, I might have lost view of the total picture. So it is important for me to prevent Steve from falling into a similar situation. I want to do it before he ends up carrying the same baggage I did, which could cloud his sight before too long."

Dad decided it wouldn't be appropriate to mention their situation with the bank. "In order to better understand how our business works, I asked our accountant to provide me with our monthly sales data. I assembled a ten-year chart but couldn't figure out its erratic ups and downs. Looking at our cycles sparked a lot of unanswered questions. Steve and I decided it would be easier to look at someone else's business rather than ours.

"And that, Janet, is where we need your help. I wonder if you would be kind enough to share with us how your business works."

Janet hesitated and then said, "The decision to transfer the business to Steve is important enough to have our meeting on such short notice. If I can be of any help, I will do my best. Yet your question is too broad. Can you be more specific?"

"We would like to understand your business cycles," Dad replied.

"You have to guide me in your cycles' deal," Janet replied.

"As a good start, maybe we can look at your monthly data," Dad suggested. "Do you happen to have your monthly sales information somewhere at your office?"

"I do, but how long do you want to go back?" Janet asked.

"How about starting with two years' worth of information?" Dad asked.

"I can only get you my current year report," Janet said. "But if you want a two-year view I will have to ask my accountant."

Janet's answer seemed to put on hold the revealing of her cycles—at least until her accountant could provide it. Steve and Dad looked at each other, wondering how to proceed.

Noticing their hesitation Janet asked, "Is there anything wrong with what I just said?"

"No," they replied together, and Steve went on to explain. "We were hoping to use your monthly information for finding cycles in your business—and then comparing it to our chart."

"Well, I'm afraid we will have to wait a while," Janet replied.

They were back to square one. Then an idea sparked in Steve's mind. "Do you happen to have weekly sales figures instead? Maybe we can learn something by using them."

Janet paused for a minute before she answered. "My accountant asks me to accumulate my weekly sales figures and give him the information at the end of each month. If it is important, I think I can gather some weekly data for you."

"How many weeks can you go back?" Steve asked.

"I can definitely get you a week or two," she replied. "But beyond that it may be too difficult."

Janet looked at them and asked, "Is it important for you to have sales data, or could it be something else?"

The question took them by surprise. "I'm not sure, Janet, what do you have in mind?" Dad asked.

"Well, instead of looking for weekly sales, why can't we simply look at the customer's schedule in my appointment book? There you may find all the information you need, and I keep those books for years."

Before Dad was able to make any comment, she continued, "Since I know how important it is to you, if you delay ordering breakfast for fifteen minutes, I will be back shortly with my appointment book."

And before any of them could say anything, off she went.

A Smooth Train Ride

It was late morning. Anticipating Janet would soon be back, Dad decided to order their second breakfast. He was trying to time it for her return.

While waiting, Steve said, "What an amazing smart lady. She just gave us a different way to look at things. Rather than gathering weekly financial figures, we can simply look at her customer schedule. We were trying to use sales data to understand her cycles. But counting customers every week may give us even more valuable information to figure out how her business ticks. Maybe looking at the source of revenues is better than the after-the-fact sales."

He paused and then asked, "So, Dad, how many weeks do we need to analyze?"

"I would start with only a few weeks and see if it leads us anywhere," Dad said. "Beyond that, a thorough search will be too long, and I don't want to take much time away from Janet. She has been already kind enough to join us on her day off. Anyway, I think that we would benefit most by asking her real questions, something we couldn't do with our virtual hairdresser."

As they were talking, Janet came back and laid her appointment book on the table.

"There it is, all in front of you, my full customer schedule, week in week out. But I wasn't sure how far back you would like to go, so I brought last year's book as well."

"Janet, I really appreciate your efforts!" Dad said. "Helping two useless guys like us is more than we could ask."

Steve was not convinced if Dad was teasing Janet, or if it was simply their style of humor. Perhaps it had developed through many years of friendship.

They all looked at her appointment book. Instead of accumulating financial data they were simply counting the number of customers for each week. Dad summed up the total for the first week and it came to thirty six. They continued counting six weeks out and the numbers came as follows:

Week 1 = 36 customers
Week 2 = 34 customers
Week 3 = 35 customers
Week 4 = 34 customers
Week 5 = 37 customers
Week 6 = 35 customers

Steve quickly grabbed a sheet of paper and drew a chart, depicting Janet's weekly customer demand.

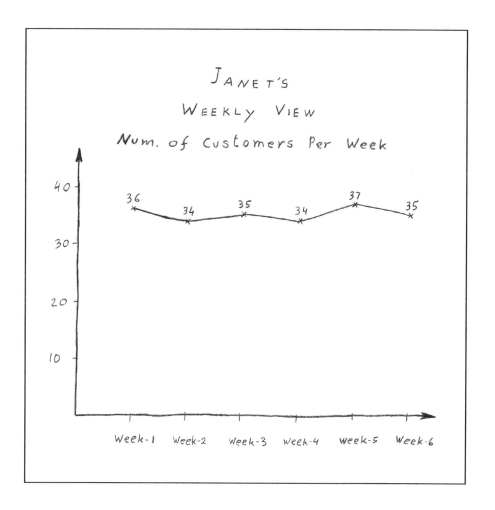

While they were busy analyzing the data, the waitress brought the breakfast to their table.

"Janet," Dad said, "Your weekly performance, at least for these six weeks, shows a pretty steady volume of work. We were expecting you would have much larger fluctuations from week to week. Can I assume if we continue looking for more weeks out, this steady pattern wouldn't change by much?"

Before Janet could answer he continued, "What does your accountant tell you at the end of each year?"

"You have asked two questions at once, so let me take them one by one," Janet replied. "My accountant tells me, 'Janet, keep up with the good work. I don't have too many customers which maintain their business in such solid form,' Janet continued with a smile, copying her accountant's Southern accent.

"And as to your other question, yes, my business is almost steady through the entire year. The only exception is at year's end when I take my annual vacation and the business is closed for the holidays".

Steve and Dad exchanged looks. Counting customers every week revealed Janet's business pattern—and it was rather steady. Janet's intuition of looking at customers in her appointment book was right. They could see the picture even without using her monthly sales figures.

Dad turned to Steve. "If we compare our ten-year chart to Janet's, it's like she's on a train crossing the big plains and we're riding on a roller coaster at a Six Flags amusement park. With its sharp turns and steep drops we may have more fun, but I'm not sure about our blood pressure."

He then looked at Janet and asked, "Wouldn't you agree with this?"

Sudden Volatility within Stability

The smell of fresh coffee and the food on their plates made them stop their serious discussion. "Let's eat before breakfast gets too cold," Dad said.

They were quiet as they began eating. Janet then asked while looking at Dad, "I think I got your roller coaster analogy, but are you saying that my business is stable and yours is not?"

"Yes I am." Dad replied. "Your appointment book and the input regarding your accountant's view, shows just that."

Janet raised her eyebrows and said, "I'm not sure you looked close enough, and even more so, I wish my business were as stable as you just described."

"I don't get it," Dad said as he pointed at her chart. "Just compare our charts and you can see the difference."

"I won't pretend to be an expert in charts, but I'm telling you that my business is at least as volatile as yours," Janet replied.

Steve could see the upcoming clash and politely said, "Excuse me for interrupting Dad, but I think Janet is trying to tell us something else."

He looked at her and asked, "Janet, could you clarify what you meant by saying we didn't look close enough?"

"Sure I can," she responded. "By comparing week by week, you concluded that my business is stable. But I'm telling you that every day is a different ball game.

"On Mondays we are usually closed. I would say Tuesday and Wednesday are relatively light. However the closer we get to the weekend, the heavier it becomes. Friday is pretty busy, but on Saturday the pressure is generally heavier. The problem with Saturday is that we can't stretch the hours. Even if we have a lot of customers we can't accommodate them all, since everybody wants to be done no later than six o'clock in the evening. So from time to time I'm forced to open at eight o'clock in the morning in order to squeeze in another customer."

Janet took a pause. "To sum it all up, unlike Saturday, on Friday we are able to stretch our time even to nine o'clock at night. But either way, these two days are normally the busiest of the week. I barely have time to eat, and I usually stay late after the last customer has left, just to put everything back in order. That's why I keep the appointment schedule very tight. Otherwise, everything seems to fall apart."

Steve glanced at Dad to see how he took it in, and then said, "Janet, it is a thorough explanation. But I wonder how it all works when you get last minute calls and walk-ins?"

"Well, yes, they do come sometimes, and I try to accommodate them as much as possible. On midweek days I have more flexibility. But since Friday and Saturday are usually booked solid, it's very seldom that I can squeeze anybody in. I try to fit them into the next week's schedule, but it only works with a few. I do my best to give priority to my most loyal customers."

Janet's heartfelt explanation confirmed that her daily business pattern was far from being stable.

Steve looked again at the appointment book, but this time he was taking an entirely different view. Instead of summing up the number of Janet's customers for the whole first week, he counted them for each day and wrote:

Tuesday = 4
Wednesday = 6
Thursday = 7
Friday = 10
Saturday = 9

Friday's figure of ten customers was two and a half times time larger than Tuesday's four.

He pointed at her weekly customer demand chart and said, "Janet, now what you said becomes very clear. The number for the lowest week was a total of thirty-four customers, while the highest was thirty-seven. It is only about ten percent variation between the lowest to the highest. However, when you look at it by the day, comparing four customers to ten is a two hundred and fifty percent variation. It's mind boggling. I wonder what happens in the following weeks?"

Steve didn't wait for an answer. He looked again at the appointment book, and counted the number of customers for a few more days. Instead of writing the figures, he plotted them on paper—with a view of two weeks. On the bottom he noted the days and marked above each day its customers' schedule. The new chart with its daily view, revealed a sight of peaks and valleys with sharp swings from high to low.

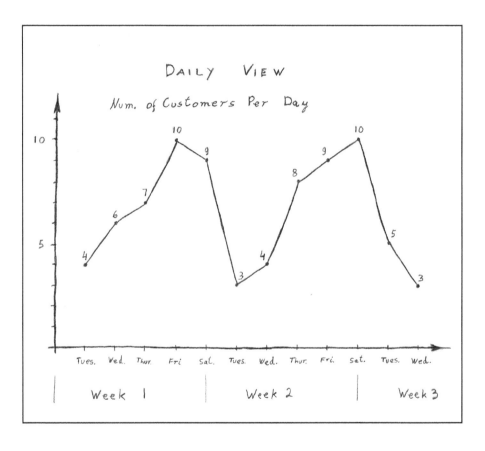

Steve turned to Dad and said, "Look how a stable week-to-week, month-to-month view, turned into a highly volatile day-to-day one. Are her swings really different from ours?"

"Now the patterns look closer," Dad admitted. "But Janet's view is only for a couple of weeks, while ours shows a ten year period," he continued still not giving up. "We must look further to see if her volatility continues, or is it only for a short while?

"Janet," Dad asked. "Can you please read me the day-by-day number of customers for a few more weeks, and then let us see if this pattern repeats itself?"

Janet read out the numbers as Dad wrote down each day's information in a table-form. He repeated it for six consecutive weeks. Then he circled the slowest day of each week and put a square over the busiest one.

	Tues.	Wed.	Thur.	Fri.	Sat.	Total
Week 1	(4)	6	7	[10]	9	36
Week 2	(3)	4	8	9	[10]	34
Week 3	5	(3)	6	[11]	10	35
Week 4	(4)	6	5	[10]	9	34
Week 5	(4)	7	6	[11]	9	37
Week 6	(3)	6	8	[10]	8	35

◯ – Weekly Lowest

▢ – Weekly Highest

Each week had a slow start at the beginning and became increasingly busy towards the end. Tuesday was the slowest five out of six times, and Friday was the busiest five out six times. It was easier to see that the strong volatility continued for all six weeks.

Pointing at Dad's summary table Steve interjected, "I bet if we continue looking in Janet's appointment book, we will see this volatile pattern continue for the whole year.

"You see, Dad, when we changed the time intervals of looking at days rather than weeks, it suddenly revealed a whole new perspective—I guess that's what really counts. Instead of a comfortable view of a weekly total customers' figure, where there is a little change from week to week, we have disturbing cycles with drastic swings from day to day. It seems the closer you look at time intervals, more accurately you see the real pattern of your business. It may be more volatile than what you think—so we are no longer alone on the roller coaster ride."

Dad cleared his throat. "Didn't I say you would be good at solving complex problems by drawing charts?" It was his way of accepting Steve's argument, and that Janet's business volatility is not much different from theirs.

He then asked, "Janet, now looking at your chart with its intense cycles, I have a question. What is your bottleneck?"

Dad's question was a sudden change of tack. Janet hesitated a minute, then tapped her chart and said, "Although my accountant told me how stable my business is, my intuition was telling me that I should find a better way to manage my busiest days. With your unintentional help, I realize that the fluctuation of my customer demand is bigger than I ever imagined."

184

She then looked at her watch. "Gentlemen, all my life I was scared of roller coaster rides, and that is why I never go to amusement parks. It was fascinating to see how you two cracked the puzzle, and I'm glad I was able to help. I thoroughly enjoyed your company and breakfast too. I was hoping to hear about a future wedding, and instead I got a roller coaster ride. At least by having you as my companions, I may end up enjoying amusement parks."

And Steve could imagine the three of them, sitting together, screaming happily on a most challenging roller coaster ride.

Janet stood up and gathered her belongings. "Now I'm already late for my beauty treatment, which I schedule on my day off as a little treat for myself. I intend to think about our discussion today, try to better comprehend my cycles, and think of what my bottleneck is. Maybe we can meet soon for another breakfast, and I will share my thoughts with you. Perhaps I will bring along my daughter Caroline and maybe Sharon can join us as well. Good luck to you, Steve, in adjusting to your new responsibility. I'm sure you and Dad will figure out your cycles and bottleneck as well."

With that, she kissed them goodbye and left.

Unrecorded Lost Opportunities

11:00 a.m.

Steve and Dad looked at each other and at their empty plates. The food on Janet's plate had remained almost untouched. She had claimed to be too full—probably she was watching her already slim figure.

"What a special lady," Dad said. "She was all prepared to hear social news, but we spoiled it discussing cycles. Not only was she patient with us, it appears she was interested in the concept as well. I think she even enjoyed the brainstorming too."

"Yes I agree," Steve replied. "She was on track during the entire breakfast conversation, and the way she looked at us made me feel she might even be two steps ahead. Maybe she is not an expert in tables and charts, but I could see how she was taking everything in, probably thinking of what to do with it next. Maybe she can consult us in figuring out our cycles too," he added smiling.

There were no customers left at the restaurant beside Dad and Steve, who were still very busy in solving the mystery of cycles. Janet's business had already unveiled a surprising volatility within assumed stability. They were not sure what surprise could be awaiting them. Nevertheless, they realized their complex situation would no longer allow them to view their business in the same light as just a few hours ago. The waiters were busy in preparation for lunch. It was an unusual time for diners to be still sitting in, and the restaurant ambiance made Dad and Steve lower their voices while continuing their intense discussion.

"It looks as if the more we dig into what we thought was a simple example, the more complicated it becomes," Dad said. "But I don't think we are done. Having Janet with us helped in understanding what happens during the week. We discovered her cycles with big swings, week in and week out. Yet, it also revealed something else."

Surprised by Dad words Steve jumped in, "I thought we covered it all. What did we miss?"

"I don't think we fully understood her weekend dilemma," Dad replied.

"I don't get it," Steve said.

Dad pointed at the six weeks table that he had made, depicting Janet's daily workload, and asked, "What happens with a customer when a weekend schedule is full, and the request cannot be met?"

"I guess Janet would offer an alternative time," Steve responded. "And if I take the customer side, I'm not sure I'll be satisfied with..."

"That's exactly what I mean," Dad said, cutting off Steve's train of thought. "It lies in customer demand, and I'm not sure we got its full view in Janet's case."

Steve looked at Dad, unable to comprehend. "Isn't it what we talked about thus far? Didn't we base our entire analysis on her customers' demand?"

"I'm not sure we truly did," Dad answered.

"But we took our data directly from her appointment book. Isn't it the source for capturing her real demand?" Steve asked.

"You are absolutely right for the source, Steve, but not for the result. We first asked her to get weekly sales, and she couldn't get the information. Then she came up with the brilliant idea of using her appointment book instead, and it was like finding a gold mine. However, Steve, her appointment book only reflects the customer she was able to schedule. But what about the customers she was not able to accommodate? Is it recorded anywhere?"

Before Steve had a chance to answer, Dad continued. "She said she does her best, but more often than not she has to refuse customers and push their appointment out—because of the weekend wall. We used the term customer demand, but now I understand we only captured a portion of it, which is the number of customers she was able to schedule."

He was running so fast that Steve had a hard time following the concept Dad was trying to explain. "Do you mean our conclusions about Janet's cycles are wrong?"

"No, Steve, but we couldn't see the full picture. Her appointment book, as good as it is, does not reflect her entire customer demand," Dad said.

"It is like seeing the momentum wheel from behind, as in my analogy of it going up and down the hill. Your records show what you get but they don't show what you have lost. So in reality your customer demand could be different from what you understand. To use your term, Steve, your 'bye' customer is already gone."

Steve looked at his momentum wheel sketch that was lying on the table with his other sketches and charts. "I'm not sure I fully comprehend your example, Dad."

"Since Janet is not with us now, I will try to explain it in general terms," Dad said.

He took a deep breath. "Imagine a customer calls on Thursday, asking for treatment on the upcoming Saturday. The hairdresser looks at her appointment book and unfortunately she is already fully booked. She then offers her first opening, say next week Tuesday, as an alternative date. But the customer has the upcoming Saturday in mind since she has a planned dinner outing with her husband and a few friends. The dinner idea just came out while the customer was talking to a friend. It is not one of these events planned weeks in advance. It's just a spontaneous decision for a Saturday outing—as it happens frequently for many people.

"Now the hairdresser is faced with a dilemma. On one hand, her customer will not accept any other day but the specific Saturday. On the other hand, the appointment book is completely full. Even if she tries to stretch herself and offers Saturday at eight o'clock at night, her customer probably will not accept it since it is too late for dinner."

"So what happens then?" Steve asked.

"Well, now our hairdresser has a real problem," Dad replied. "She wants to please her customer but she can't, and the customer does not accept next week's date. The customer is likely to go to her planned dinner outing unhappy about her looks, and probably highly disappointed with her hairdresser. Her letdown may eventually make her look for another hairdresser. If I have to put myself in the hairdresser's shoes, I'm not sure I have a good solution. However, from experience there is one thing I'm sure of, Steve."

"What is it, Dad?"

"Neither our virtual hairdresser, nor Janet or anybody else would record it in their appointment book—and with the passage of time there will be no memory or real appreciation of the lost opportunity.

Greek Gods, Sisyphus and Dad

Dad's answer was interrupted by the sound of people talking. It was not loud. But the quietness of the restaurant, with only random clinking sounds of plates and silverware, amplified the conversation. Dad and Steve turned their heads as a customer walked in and asked if he could be seated for lunch. Unfortunately, the waitress had to turn his request down. It was about an hour away from serving lunch. The customer must have been very hungry and was not ready to give up.

"Is there something I can get instead? Maybe you are still serving breakfast?" he asked.

It was that time of the day that she couldn't offer breakfast or lunch. The only thing she could offer was some coffee, or he would have to return at noon. The customer mumbled and left the restaurant.

Completely taken in by the view of the customer walking out Steve said, "Dad, didn't we have just one right in front of our eyes?"

"Which one are you talking about?" Dad asked.

"A living example of a lost opportunity—the customer who was asking for an early lunch," Steve replied. "He came in but eventually was turned down and he walked out unsatisfied."

Pleased by Steve catching up with the notion, Dad said, "We don't know yet, but it wouldn't take long to find out. All we need to see is if he will be coming back for lunch. Since it seems we are going to be here for a while, we definitely will be able to record the event."

He stopped for a moment and looked around. "I bet you the waitress didn't record it anywhere—and if the customer doesn't come back, the opportunity may not be lost only once."

"What do you mean by losing more than once?" Steve asked.

"Well, first, we would have an immediate loss of lunch income," Dad explained. "Second, we would have an unhappy customer who may not come back at all. What is even worse, he may pass the word around, causing others not to come."

Before Steve could respond, Dad continued. "What's sad is that Jim would never know about the incident—and how much potential business had been lost. Even sadder, it all happened when the restaurant was almost empty."

The possibility of having a lost opportunity when things are slow hit Steve hard. Immediately he took it to their discussion on Janet. "We discussed her weekend dilemma when she is overloaded. But can it happen in other days of the week when she is less busy?"

"Didn't you ask her about walk-in and last minute calls?" Dad replied. "Think of a walk-in situation during her less busy days. A customer comes in and asks for a hairdo. I bet Janet would quickly suggest the next available opening. If the waiting time is not too long, the customer will wait and eventually get the service and everybody is happy. The customer for being accepted, the hairdresser for getting more business, and the unexpected demand is captured in her appointment book.

"However, what happens if the wait is too long and the customer decides to leave?" Dad asked.

He didn't wait for an answer and continued, "Janet may be below her daily capacity, and yet she may not be able to capture a walk-in opportunity because of the waiting time. In such a case there is no record of the event, and her appointment book will not reflect the loss. So Steve, the old saying of timing is everything applies here in full. It is as if we are looking on a Tuesday schedule in Janet's appointment book with say, only five customers, and interpret it as her actual demand. While being well below capacity, she might have lost a customer or two on that day.

Dad took a breath. "And it does not end here. I can see a last minute call and all sorts of customers' special requirements that can challenge her ability to respond, and eventually cause lost opportunities. I know that she would do her best to work things around, but as she becomes busier, her ability to be flexible lessens."

Sitting in the quiet restaurant Steve then asked, "Dad, the more we talk about it, the scarier it gets. I wonder how many lost customers are out there—and how do they affect cycles?"

"That's a double whammy question," Dad replied. "Since you can't find lost opportunities in any appointment book or financial logs, there is no accurate way to calculate it. You are usually so busy with day-to-day issues that your mind does not capture the magnitude of the loss. You feel it. You know it is there. But you don't know its exact size. Intuitively you know you lost, but psychologically you comfort yourself saying 'It probably wasn't too much,' or 'I couldn't do much about it.'

"Unfortunately, lost opportunities do happen all too often and their value could be bigger than you imagine. Maybe you can make an educated estimate, but I wonder how close to reality such an estimate would be."

Steve could no longer contain his excitement. "So, Dad, how many lost opportunities do we have?"

He then placed Dad's chart in the center of the table. "Here in front of us we have our own monthly chart, and it is extremely abrupt. It is like climbing up and then, without warning, falling—and it happens over and over...."

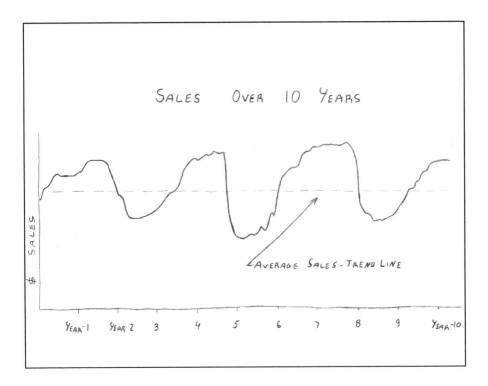

Pointing at the volatile line he said, "Dad what is the nature of our cycles? Could their volatile pattern be because of our lost opportunities?"

Dad looked at Steve and sighed. "Did I ever tell you the story of Sisyphus?"

Before Steve could answer, he continued. "In Greek mythology, Sisyphus' punishment from the gods was to roll a huge rock to the top of a mountain. As he was just a step away from the peak, the rock would fall back, only for Sisyphus to push it up for eternity—and start all over again. The story itself goes far beyond that. But for most people, similar hurdles in life that seem insurmountable are called a 'Sisyphean task.' Looking back, I have to admit that it often felt like I was pushing the weight of our business up the hill. When I finally filled our shop with customers' orders and enjoyed nice profits for a while, it did not take long to slip back—only to start all over again. When I told you, Steve, about my bottleneck search and what came after, now I understand that it was just one cycle out of many. Our ten-year sales history, as it is depicted on this chart, substantiated that I wasn't entirely wrong with what I had felt. Yes, the chart doesn't reflect our lost opportunities—probably too many to count. And I have no idea how much loss was there...."

There was silence for a moment or two. Then Dad added, "I'm not going to be here for eternity and we must find the answer to the pattern of our cycles—so you will not have to push up that rock and fall back as well."

In order to lighten the conversation he added with a hint of a smile, "You know, Steve, maybe that is the destiny of people who enjoy their work and become craftsmen in their trade."

"But you shouldn't despair," Dad continued. "The French author and philosopher Albert Camus, a Nobel Prize winner in literature, suggested in the conclusion of his essay The Myth of Sisyphus: 'The struggle itself toward the heights is enough to fill a man's heart. One must imagine Sisyphus happy.'

With Dad's positive note, Steve could picture in his mind Dad and him pushing the rock uphill singing happily out loud.

Drink Wine and Have a Strong Heart

Steve and Dad were so focused that they did not even notice Dad's old friend Jim, the restaurant owner, standing near their table. "Hello, old friends. I just got in and what a pleasant surprise. It must be a special occasion—I normally see you here for dinner. Are you in for a late breakfast or an early lunch? Since you are the only guests around, I can personally prepare you a nice brunch," Jim added with a smile.

Jim was known to have a sharp sense of humor mixed with some cynicism and a very big heart. You couldn't stay angry with him for too long when he teased you, and in the end he would give a wink with his big laugh.

Dad and Steve couldn't believe it was almost noon.

"I guess time does fly when you're having fun," Dad responded. "And you are right, Jim, we do have a special occasion, although it is yet far from celebration time. Yesterday I told Steve about my decision to hand over our business to him, and he ended up not getting a wink of sleep all night. We have already had a second breakfast but more coffee will do just fine. I will take a rain check for brunch. We have so much to cover and the way things are progressing here we may as well stay for dinner—perhaps even ask our ladies to join us."

"Is my lady included?" Jim asked with a laugh as he left to make fresh coffee.

"Knowing Jim, he will return with some good cookies as well," Dad said. "I better watch my diet; it's going to be a long day."

"I would avoid cookies too," Steve said. He then lowered his voice and asked, "Dad, does Jim know about our situation with the Bank?"

"Why do you ask?" Dad replied.

"I thought that if he is in the loop we can tell him about Mr. Bupti and get his read on it," Steve answered. "Sometimes you never know—with all the people who come here to dine, maybe Jim also knows Mr. Bupti's relatives."

Surprised by Steve's change of tack Dad answered, "Yes, I have asked for Jim's help, although I didn't have a chance to tell him about the urgent meeting at the bank. But even so, what would you do if Jim knew Mr. Bupti's relatives?

"Maybe we can talk to them," Steve replied. "If nothing else we may get a little more knowledge of who he is."

"It's not a bad idea, but I have a hunch we will know sooner than later," Dad responded.

Jim coming to the scene and the divergence in their conversation helped them put aside uphill-rock-pushing melancholy, guilt trips and soul searching. Dad and Steve were back on track.

"Dad, we have in front of us three different charts," Steve said. "The first deals with seasonality cycles with unpredictable swings. The second is

Janet's, where we found erratic cycles and disturbing unrecorded lost opportunities. The last is ours with its harsh peaks and valleys. It seems we have randomness and instability all over the place, and we don't yet have a clue if we also have hidden cycles. I believe that if we do, they are at least as unstable as in Janet's case."

As they were talking, Jim came back with coffee and cookies.

"It's a pre-lunch break now—so why don't you guys stop for a moment, step away from your serious conversation, and enjoy yourselves," Jim said as he poured fresh coffee for them. Not wanting to offend Jim they each took a cookie. Even though they were full, they broke off a few bits and chewed them slowly.

"I hope you will excuse me for being nosy," Jim continued. "When I first came in, I heard you talking about cycles. I left you for a little while, and when I came back, guess what? You're still talking cycles."

He looked at Dad. "What in the world is this all about? Is this your way to keep Steve awake after you caused him to lose sleep all night? I'm sure my coffee and cookies would do a much better job."

Knowing all too well Jim's unique humorous style, Dad went along with it. "You see Jim, it is this chart's fault," and he showed his ten-year chart pointing at it peaks and valleys. "That is why we are sitting here discussing cycles and bottlenecks. I got the idea of plotting it from an article I read long ago. So look what we got—up and down swings in a random pattern. We can't find any predictability. And Jim, I don't have to tell you what happens when you are on a rocky ride. I wonder how your chart would look if we plotted your business behavior back a few years."

Jim chuckled. "If I take your advice and chart my cycles for ten years, not only will it take that long to prepare, but I would probably need a thousand pages just to fit it in. In my business, I have swings three times a day. It happens every morning when customers arrive for breakfast—and then my restaurant empties. It happens again at lunch and is repeated at every dinner—and each time it happens I have no idea what to expect."

"Excuse me, Jim," Dad interjected. "But I don't see what is there to expect. You have breakfast and then lunch followed by dinner, so what is the problem?"

"Well, I guess I didn't make myself clear," Jim answered. "I have no idea what is coming in. I purchase products and prepare my staff not knowing if the lunch today is going to be full or if we will be sitting idly by. Will dinner tonight reach full capacity and we will be running around like crazy, trying to provide speedy service to impatient customers, or will the place be nearly deserted? I have no predictability—none whatsoever from meal to meal, let alone from day to day.

"That's why in my business you drink a lot of wine and need to have a strong heart," and he burst out laughing.

Retaining his wit Jim looked closely at Dad's chart, "I bet depicting a one-day behavior at my restaurant, could fluctuate like your entire ten years, if not even more. We never know what is going to happen within a few hours. I serve people when they come to dine, and you service tools at your shop. We are both in the service business, but at least your tools don't yell at you when they are not satisfied."

Dad was getting ready to answer, but Jim was unstoppable. "And just to show you how running a restaurant is hell, let me tell you a joke: If you know somebody that you don't like, wish him to be in the restaurant business. And if you really dislike him, wish him great on-going success."

Dad couldn't hold back his laughter. But very quickly he got back to his usual form, and said in his somewhat dry manner. "If I were to tell you about my day, you would see it is not much different from yours. Behind every tool there is an impatient customer who wants it back right away. So Jim you are right. My tools don't yell at me, but the customers who own them do—whenever they are not happy with my service. Because you are in the direct service world, you can at least calm your unhappy customer with an apology, a smile, and a small gesture too.

"More than that," Dad continued. "If you were to look at the way tools come into my shop during the day, you would find great volatility from hour to hour. Sometimes in three hours nothing comes in and we may have nothing to work on. But in the fourth hour we could end up with a load of tools that would take two days of work to service. So tell me, Jim, who has greater stress and who has higher work volatility—you or me? At least you have regular breaks and time intervals between meals, thus you can better schedule your day."

Jim did not laugh this time. "You have a good point. Perhaps your business and mine are not much different after all."

Listening to their intense talk Steve thought, "I guess it is good that two old friends argue from time to time. Jim's spontaneous involvement with our conversation has challenged Dad so much, that he did not even real-ize he was taking his first cut at revealing our daily cycles—and they seem even more chaotic than I could ever have imagined."

Their conversation was interrupted by the chef asking Jim to come to the kitchen. He politely excused himself.

Response Time with Dad's Friends

As Jim left, Dad looked at the cookie plate, and it was empty. "Steve, did you eat any of the cookies?"

"No, I didn't have any."

"Did you see Jim taking any?" Dad asked.

Steve laughed, "He was standing here the entire time and you did not even ask him to join us. I did not see his long hand reaching for the cookie plate, so I wonder how they could have disappeared."

"Damn," Dad said. "I couldn't have eaten them all. Maybe we should skip lunch; otherwise, I will have to starve for the next two days just to balance out my excess intake. Please don't tell Mom. I promised her I'd stick to my strict diet."

"I won't tell her," Steve replied. "But you will have to deal with Jim, since I believe he is doing his best to restore the peace between you two by preparing lunch for us. We tested Janet's patience today; I'm not sure you want to test Jim's."

"What do you suggest I do?" Dad asked.

"I think that after today you should starve for three days," Steve answered with a laugh. "With the rate food is coming in, maybe I should starve with you too—but at least we should enjoy today. Now that we have resolved our diet balance issues, can we switch back from cookies to cycles?"

"Sure we can, although cookies are much sweeter," Dad said, keeping his humor as well.

"Dad, which of your friends are we going to meet next?"

The question sounded so out of context that Dad wasn't sure if Steve was joking. "I don't have anyone in mind. Why do you ask?"

"We started with Janet, and we discovered how much her daily schedule fluctuates," Steve answered. "Then we talked to Jim, and we suddenly have customer demand fluctuating by the hour—suggesting hourly cycles within the day. Maybe your next friend will unfold cycles of minutes within the hour, and the next one would show us oscillations of seconds within the minute."

"Now I see what you mean, Steve—it is like zooming in. The closer you look, the more cycles are revealed."

Dad then in a more serious tone said, "Thinking about it, maybe we should talk to my friend Bob, who is an expert in the telephone and communication business. There, things happen in matter of a split second. I'm sure he could definitely tell us how an influx of a thousand calls coming in, have to be instantly channeled in order to satisfy all customers simultaneously."

"I was just trying to make a point," Steve replied. "Before taking my suggestion too literally, I think we can stop here. I suggest we go back to our business, before we dig into nuclear physics and cycles of nanoseconds—with the help of another one of your many friends," he summed it up with a smile.

"I can get my pal John to cover this subject too," Dad said, going along with Steve. "But don't worry—not all of my friends are having a day off to join us here. Anyway, we have too much on our plate, and I don't mean just food."

"Dad, I think you have highlighted a critical point," Steve said.

"And what might that be?" Dad asked.

"That no matter where you are in your cycle—high or low—you must always keep your response intact," Steve answered.

"I don't follow," Dad raised a brow.

Steve realized that perhaps his wording had become too academic. "Let me explain Dad. In your example of Bob, a thousand calls are needed to be channeled in a split second in order to satisfy all customers. So, a random peak of demand must receive instant service response—and the customer will not accept any delay. There, at all time, the expected response time to receiving service is nil."

Steve paused and then asked, "Dad, what did Jim say regarding the required service time for his customers?"

"I don't recall him mentioning anything specific about his service time," Dad answered.

"You're right Dad," Steve replied. "Jim didn't specify service time. But, I thought he said that whenever he ends up reaching full capacity, he and his staff will start running around like crazy, trying to provide speedy service to impatient customers. Then, how quickly must he respond?"

He took a breath and continued. "In running any business, there is the customer demand on one side, and on the other, the ability to fulfill it. However, things start to get complicated when they don't match. Whenever your capacity is full or for whatever reason you are not able to provide the service, you are forced to push the customer out.

"Can you imagine what would happen in Bob's case, if instead of getting an instant telephone connection, a customer would have to stay on the line for an hour? And what would happen with Janet, if she would have to push a customer out for two to three weeks? I'm almost sure she would lose the sale—if not eventually the customer. So business owners like Janet, Jim, we, and others, must have a measurement or a guideline defining their maximum leeway in stretching out service response time."

"What would you say is that magical number, Steve?" Dad asked.

"I'm not sure, Dad, but that is what we need to find out. Maybe for Janet it is a couple of days or maybe even a week. Beyond that, I think it will be challenging her customers' patience. That doesn't include walk-in customers, who will not wait for even an hour. But wouldn't it be best if we were to simply ask her?"

An Unwritten Rule of Expectations

1:00 p.m.

Dad and Steve were so preoccupied discussing response time, that they had not noticed the hum of people almost filling the restaurant to full capacity.

As Dad was talking, Jim walked over to their table with his great smile. "Gentlemen, your lunch is ready and—surprise, surprise!—it is not something you ordered. I prepared something special you simply cannot refuse."

He then looked at Steve and said with a grin, "I hope my coffee kept you wide awake, since I know your father can become too serious and dry. By the way, was it you, Steve, who finished the cookies? I know your dad is on a strict diet on your Mom's orders."

Taking lightly Jim's comment Dad said, "Steve asked me a question about your business that I'm sure I can't answer, but maybe you can. I have an idea—why don't you join us for lunch, Jim? I know it is an unusual request, but I hope you will honor us for this special occasion of Steve's promotion as the new company head. We have decided to skip diet-watching for today, so maybe you can join the feast as well," hinting at Jim's somewhat rotund appearance.

"Here they go, starting to butt heads again," Steve thought. But to his surprise the always busy Jim accepted the invitation right away.

"The restaurant is filling up, but I can ask my staff to keep an eye on my other guests. Just give me a minute, and I will be joining you guys. It has been a long time since I was served in my own restaurant. Maybe while joining you, I can check the quality of our service from the other side."

As Jim left, Steve said, "I need to stretch for a minute," and stood up.

"Why don't we both take a short break until Jim joins us? I can give Mom a call," Dad suggested.

"It's a good idea, I will talk to Sharon as well," Steve said.

A few minutes later they came back to the table where Jim was already sitting. "What took you so long?" he said. "I was worried I would have to eat my meal and yours as well," he chuckled.

The first course was quickly served.

"Steve has a question regarding your service," Dad said. "I bet you will probably impress us with your fast response."

"What do you mean?" Jim asked.

"That is exactly Steve's question," Dad replied. "What response do your customers expect?"

"Well, I'm sure they want to see my smiling face welcoming them in, getting some good food, and a drink or two with a joke included; that is the standard I demand from my staff as well," Jim answered.

"But of course," Dad said. "And how long are your customers willing to wait?"

Instead of answering, Jim asked, "Before, during, or after?"

In spite of strict table manners Steve jumped in. "I got what Jim means. We need to know what the expected wait is, throughout the entire service cycle. From the moment a customer walks in until he leaves."

"My customers expect immediate response—there are no ifs, ands, or buts about it," Jim said. "Everybody wants to be seated without waiting, but it does not mean I can always accommodate their request. Whenever we get busy, as the restaurant is filling up, they do have to wait a little."

"How long does it take before a customer becomes a little edgy?" Steve inquired.

"Well, I guess it varies," Jim replied. "Everyone has his own time limit, but I would say waiting fifteen to twenty minutes when we are full, is probably when people's patience is put to the test. If it's more than that, I know we are in serious trouble. Then, most people lose their patience and go somewhere else."

"This covers the 'before' part of your answer, Jim," Steve said. "It is only the beginning of the cycle, when people arrive just before being seated. But what happens throughout the 'during' portion—from the moment they have been seated until the moment they finish eating?"

"Well, it's a multi step process," Jim explained. "But as a general rule, Steve, I would say that waiting up to fifteen minutes for service is the limit. Beyond that, people will probably become really upset."

"Do they then just get up and leave?" Steve asked.

"In most cases they don't, but some of them either openly express dissatisfaction or subtly let you know. What worries me most is that I could possibly lose them as returning customers—especially those who didn't say anything."

"And to finish your service cycle, Jim, what happens after?"

"After the customers finish eating, they ask for the check. There, I would say, fifteen minutes becomes much too long. People are done with their dinner, and they want to leave as soon as possible. If for some reason they are delayed, I'm running the risk of an unhappy customer, and you never know the implications," Jim sighed. "The whole process is so fragile, and you have to be on top of everything all the time—and I'm only a single person in the battle."

Steve wondered if Dad had ever seen Jim so serious. Jim, the one of everlasting humor, seemed very much like Dad: all at once serious and deep in thought, similar in posture and presence as Dad was when he had discussed his escaping cycles and bottleneck search.

He then thought, "I can add him to the picture of Dad and I—all of us together pushing the rock uphill"

Jim looked at Dad and poured wine in their glasses. "Remember my joke; that running a restaurant is hell? I would like to take this special opportunity and make a toast to our strong hearts; and Steve's welcome to the club." Jim was coming back to his usual humorous self.

"I'm fine with the wine, but we will delay the formal announcement about Steve's future," Dad said.

Needless to say, Jim's special lunch was outstanding. While enjoying food and conversation, Steve could tell that Jim's eyes were constantly checking on his staff—for the service they provided to his other customers.

"I wonder if he is measuring the response time to fulfill customers' expectations," Steve thought to himself.

Steve then asked, "Based on what you said, Jim, it looks as though every time you cross the fifteen- to twenty-minute mark, you are at risk of losing business. Does this expected response time figure pertain only to your place, or is it the norm for the entire restaurant industry?"

Jim took another sip of his wine and answered, "I guess it is an unwritten rule. It's not something I've scientifically studied, but my guess would be that if you were to talk to many restaurant owners you will get a similar answer. However, like everything in life, I believe there are a few exceptions. One is the fast food business, where I believe the expected response time is less than half—maybe five to ten minutes range. Another exception is the upscale restaurant scene, where anything goes. I know of places where you have to make reservation weeks—and sometimes months—in advance. In which case, I can imagine that while eating and afterward, people's patience is endless. But for the majority of restaurants like ours, the range I have given you is the norm."

He then looked at Dad and Steve. "You dine here a lot and in many other places—why don't you ask yourselves, as customers, what is your expected response time?"

Waiting in Line at Jim's Place

Dad and Steve were quiet for a minute, trying to come up with an answer to what would test their limit of patience for waiting time.

Their thoughts were interrupted by Jim. "What is taking you so long?" he teased them. "I thought frequent diners like you would instantly have the answer."

"I guess it varies by a personal point of view, but I expect the response time to be shorter—ten minutes max," Steve replied. "Is that your opinion too, Dad?"

"Maybe I'm old school, but I can live with fifteen minutes waiting time and maybe a little more." Dad answered. "I also agree with Jim's estimates for the fast food business and upscale restaurants—but with only one exception. Recently I read about a most prestigious restaurant in Europe where a meal is so sought after, that the waiting time is over a year, and you can't even choose your meal. You just have to accept whatever the chef prepares for the day and the price is fixed at four hundred Euros per person. The successful chef is so tired after many years, that although he announced closing the place for a whole year, there are already enough reservations for when he comes back."

Dad looked at Jim. "Now back to our humble reality. Since I never saw you using a stop watch clocking people coming in, how do you measure the waiting-time?"

"Well, I monitor the line of people waiting to be seated," Jim answered. "You use your intuition as a measuring tool."

"And what about the waiting time during and after the meal—how do you monitor it?" Dad inquired.

"That is much more difficult. I guess the only way I can evaluate it, is by the amount of orders piling up in the kitchen and the way my staff runs around. Over the years you develop your intuition to weigh up these types of situations," Jim answered.

"So Jim, it looks as though you have built an intuitive gauge," Dad said.

"You are probably right. But more often than not it feels the gauge is behind and things begin to slip up," Jim sighed.

"I see," Dad said. "So when things get busy and the waiting line is extended to twenty minutes or more, what do you do then?"

"I tell people to hold on to their hunger, until next day's meal, promising they will be the first to be served," Jim joked.

He then changed his tone, "As I told you already, people become uneasy and even begin to leave. It's a most frustrating situation."

Dad and Steve exchanged glances as the 'bye' customer situation—earlier at the restaurant—came back to mind. "Jim, it is in such situations that you have lost opportunities, and I bet they are not recorded anywhere," Dad said.

Jim shook his head. "What do you mean by that?"

Dad then shared the whole notion of lost opportunities with Jim. He was ready to tell him about the customer who had just walked in, and then in frustration walked out. It was a perfect example to demonstrate a lost opportunity. Yet he decided not to bring it up, as he felt that it could easily make Jim upset with his staff. He knew that Jim would get furious if he knew the customer had left, while the restaurant was practically empty.

Instead Dad asked, "How often do you find yourself faced with extended waiting times, and do you keep any records of such days?"

Jim looked at Dad, astounded. "What in the world for? Why would I do that?"

"To get an idea of how much business you lose and find if there is any connection to your cycles," Dad answered.

Jim was quiet for a minute. Dad's proposition gave it a whole new twist. "I think I begin to see your point, but I have no idea how to go back in time and figure it all out." He hesitated a little and then said, "Are there any suggestions?"

"Maybe we can look at your financial information," Dad replied. "There must be some records that would indicate your workload. Maybe when it was heavy, the service time had slackened off—leading to a long waiting time and unhappy customers."

Jim took it in. "Possibly our daily revenue could reflect just that. It's not an accurate measurement, as the figures may fluctuate depending on what people order for their meal. But in general, the higher the revenues the busier we become."

"Jim, it's an excellent idea and we can use it as a good start," Dad responded. "Yet, I'm afraid it's not sufficient to figure out your lost opportunities and cycles. They seem to fluctuate by the shift, instead of by the day. Didn't you say that situations of long waiting time randomly happened from shift to shift?"

He then continued, "So do you have any records for the shift?"

"You have a lot of tough questions today," Jim replied disappointedly. "I'm afraid we don't."

Dad exchanged looks with Steve as though he was trying to communicate with him that once more they were stuck.

Paper Napkin with an Untold Story Behind It

Lunchtime passed its peak and the restaurant was emptying. The second cycle of the day in Jim's place was diminishing while his staff was busy cleaning up.

Steve, who was quietly listening to the entire conversation, interjected, "Excuse me for interrupting. Jim, is there anything that may show how many people come to dine in every shift? It can provide us with an idea of how much business might have been lost—and how much more can be gained."

Jim scratched his head while thinking about Steve's notion. He then said. "I have an idea. We note reservations on our weekly calendar, and we add walk-in customers as we fill in our tables. However, we only keep the information for a few days."

There was a sigh of relief by father and son. As it was with Janet, it showed that asking a good question can trigger even a better answer. Jim just opened the door for connecting his cycles with lost opportunities.

"Even a few days can be a good start to portray the pattern of your cycles," Steve said. "Instead of just relying on intuition, you would have solid data and maybe it can help in recognizing new opportunities."

"Now my curiosity is peaked," Jim responded. "I will get the information very soon."

The three finished their meal and Jim summed things up.

"It has been a long time since I had the opportunity to relax in my own restaurant, eat good food, and drink wine. It definitely brought a different angle, being served while discussing required response time and cycles too. While eating, I couldn't help but watch my staff from a customer's point of view. Also it gave me an opportunity to think of your notion about unrecorded lost opportunities, which I will try to capture before long.

"Gentlemen, I very much enjoyed your company. Now please excuse me, as I feel like a captain who abandoned his ship. I need to check on the kitchen and deal with staff issues, but I will be back with some dessert very soon."

As he was ready to leave, Dad said, "Please don't—maybe later, I must stick to my diet."

"So be it," Jim chuckled. "But I will come back to check on you soon and bring some fresh coffee as well." As he was heading toward the kitchen, Steve called out after him. "Hey Jim, can I ask you for a small favor?"

"Ok Steve, I guess it is about the dessert. Would you like any special frosting on your cake?" Jim asked with a wink.

"Maybe that as well," Steve replied. "But I wonder, as you gather the number of people who dined here in the past few days, can you note which was breakfast, lunch, and dinner?"

"Asking for special frosting and unusual notes? You really are getting spoiled," Jim said with a smile.

"I have an idea, I will bring our calendar over so you can sum it up any way you choose," Jim added. "But I'm afraid I cannot do it now since the seating log is in use until the shift is over."

He then got a glimpse of disappointment on Steve's face and mumbled, "Oh well. I will see what I can do for you," and quickly left.

Steve turned to Dad and said, "I can't wait to see what pattern will be revealed."

Within just a few minutes Jim came back with fresh coffee, put it on the table and said, "Here it is. I couldn't find a decent piece of paper, so I wrote the figures you'd asked me on a napkin instead. It captures the last three days and this morning's information only. I can't give you today's lunch yet, since we may still have an additional guest or two."

He handed Steve the paper napkin and asked, "Is my handwriting legible?"

"I see the numbers very clearly, but can you verify which figure relates to its specific shift?" Steve answered.

"I'm sorry; I put the figures sequentially without notation. The first one of twenty-eight diners is breakfast three days ago. The next one of forty-eight is lunch, and so on by each shift, until today's breakfast."

28
48
41
42
34
51
43
32
50
44

"Thanks Jim," Steve said and noted the shifts next to each figure.

He looked at the paper napkin and scanned the figures a few times, trying to find a hidden pattern within. He then asked, "I see three times where the numbers are around fifty. Was the restaurant full on those shifts?"

"You can say that," Jim answered. "Whenever we have over forty diners, things get really busy here. Sometimes it even becomes difficult to fit the next guests in."

"Why is that, Jim? Didn't you just say that at about fifty is where your capacity is full?" Steve asked.

"Imagine we have forty-five diners and a group of, say, six people, comes in. It may become a challenge to find them an available table, and they may have to wait until we can seat them together," Jim explained. "You know, it's a matter of timing and party size to fill all our tables."

"So if I understand it correctly Jim, whenever you come close to seating capacity, you may still have people waiting, even if you have a few seats available," Steve said.

"Well of course, Steve. Would you like a seat at a table with people you don't know?" Jim chuckled. "You probably would, but I'm not sure about the other party," and laughed.

He then continued. "Seriously, it's all related to tables' arrangement and the combination of arriving parties. Thinking about it, we may have only forty people dining, and yet a line of people will be forming in at our reception area."

"So can you say that the closer you get to seating capacity, the longer the line will be?" Steve asked.

"In most cases that's what happens. The art of fitting people into tables—where they all will be happy—becomes a big challenge every time."

"So in such cases, do you have any idea of how many wouldn't wait in line and leave?" Steve asked.

"That's a tough question," Jim said thoughtfully. "Some people may not even join the line when they see it's too long, and simply skip to the next restaurant they find. Also, there are those who would change their minds and leave after a few minutes' wait. So, Steve, your guess is as good as mine."

Jim looked around, "Please excuse me now, but I really need to get back to check on a few things." And he was gone.

Dad was quiet for a moment or two. He then pointed at the paper napkin. "With Jim's figures we may be able to draw his cycles, but it looks as though his serving capacity is a moving number. I guess figuring out his lost opportunities may be harder than I initially imagined...."

Steve could sense Dad's mind bridging from Jim's case into their business, trying to figure out what their own lost opportunities might be.

Coming back from being in deep thought, Dad said, "Anyway Steve, let's plot Jim's shift by shift chart so we can have some idea how his cycles work."

Steve pulled out a clean sheet of paper and started drawing a new chart. On the bottom he marked the shifts during the day, and for each meal he wrote the number of people who came to dine—according to the data on

Jim's napkin. He then connected all of the marked points, depicting Jim's cycles within three days plus a morning shift—forming a wave like pattern with high peaks and low troughs.

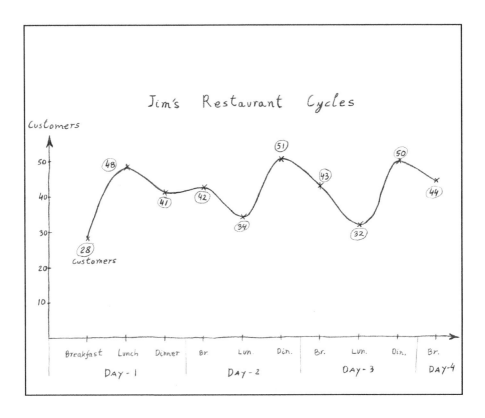

"Dad, look at Jim's swings," Steve said as he was pointing at the chart. "On one morning, only twenty-eight customers came to dine and a few hours later forty-eight showed for lunch—that's a huge swing within only a few hours. Then hours later he had forty-one for dinner and so on. I bet the volatility would persist even if we extend the view and plot a few more weeks."

Not letting Dad respond, he continued, "It is only one part of the story, which is already bad enough. But each shift's number of people who came to dine, could be holding an untold story behind it."

"Steve, you are going too fast," Dad interrupted.

But Steve was unstoppable. His excitement was as high as if he was actually running the restaurant.

"What do you do with your staff when you have only twenty-eight customers at breakfast and a few hours later you have forty-eight at lunch? Do you let your staff be partially idle in the morning, or do you send some home?

"And what do you do at noon when your people are running around like they're in a war zone? Do you add a few, or just let your service fall behind? What do you do when things may slow down again at dinner?

He pointed at the paper napkin with Jim's figures and said, "How do you manage your resources with such big swings? What happens to your service then? Do customers get seated quickly enough? Are they served in less than fifteen minutes—their expected service time?

"This is what I meant, Dad, in the untold story behind each shift; without even getting into the lost opportunities tale. Anticipating each meal is like spinning the casino's roulette wheel. You know which number you want to get but almost never do. The numbers always appear to be at random."

Steve then switched back into their reality. "Dad, arguing with Jim whose daily cycles are worse, tells me that we are in the same boat as him. As you said, in our business there is a customer behind every tool we service. So in essence, we could have expanding lines of customers waiting for their orders as well. We expect Jim to find his lost opportunities, yet we don't even know how many we had."

He sighed. "Now it's clear why Jim said running a restaurant is hell: how do you manage to get around such swings? Maybe we should be joining him too. No wonder you need a strong heart—and a lot of wine too."

Dad was quiet. He put his ten-year chart next to Jim's shift-by-shift graph and said, "I don't mind having some wine but I don't like gambling, and it may be the reason why I don't own a restaurant. Nevertheless we, like Jim, and too many others have such rocky cycles—that we are not even fully aware of their impact on our lives. This brings us back to your blindfolded captain, Steve. We can't ignore the erratic cycles and just carry on. So, drinking wine will remain only for fun and not for blindfolding the eyes."

He was ready to carry on, but had to stop. "Gentlemen excuse me for interrupting, but I really like that idea," Jim said, as he was approaching their table.

Flexing Capacity

Dad and Steve turned their heads surprised. "Jim, which idea are you talking about?" Dad asked.

"I heard you talking about joining me for wine, but what is it with blind-folding the eyes," Jim laughed. "Actually, I just came to check on you guys. Why the long faces?"

"We're discussing some serious matters pertaining to the future of our business—hence the long faces," Dad said.

"I'm sure the future is guaranteed when you hand over the business to Steve," Jim said.

"I'm sure of that too, and it is why we are still here. However, with your brainstorming skills we feel you can pull us out," Dad smiled.

"I'm flattered by your suggestion, but you are the expert here," Jim replied. "And by the way, what did you do to my napkin?"

Before Jim continued, Steve cut in. "I am glad you just came by. We figured out your cycles Jim, and we need your input." He showed Jim the chart he made.

Jim examined it for a minute and said, "It is impressive, but it looks as though you have designed a new roller coaster. Is this your new hobby, Steve?"

"No, it's not," Steve answered, laughing. "I simply plotted your shift-by-shift data, noting the number of people who came to dine, and by the way here is your napkin, Jim."

"So what did you figure out?" Jim asked.

"Now that you have your chart, Dad says you have to face the wave with your eyes wide open."

Jim shook his head. "Have you guys been drinking something other than the glass of wine we had at lunch? I already brought you coffee to overcome even that small amount. What are you hiding under the table?" Dramatically, he bent down lifting the tablecloth like he was searching for a hidden bottle of whisky.

"All we had is just your coffee, Jim. But looking at your chart, can make anyone feel dizzy even without any drink," Dad replied with a laugh.

He pointed at the second figure on Jim's graph. Changing his tone of voice, Dad said, "Now getting more serious Jim, right there you were heavily loaded with forty-eight guests for lunch. How many lost opportunities did you have then?"

Jim hesitated. "Your guess is as good as mine."

"So how would you react, if I say that there were eight people who left because of a long wait?" Dad continued.

"Is this a theoretical number or is this for real?" Jim asked, surprised by Dad's estimate.

"I don't know if it is for real since it's not recorded anywhere," Dad answered. "But even fewer than eight it's bad enough. So what would you do in such a case?"

"Before I answer I need to clarify if you are referring to a one-time loss or repeated one?" Jim said.

"You told us that customer's loss could happen every time you have over forty guests in one shift," Dad replied. "And according to your chart, it occurred seven out of the last ten times. So Jim, can you estimate how many customers have been lost within the last three days?"

Jim looked at the chart. "I don't have any idea, but every customer loss within any shift is intolerable. And if it's repeated whenever I'm maxing out, it must be a disastrous amount."

"So what do you intend to do about it, Jim?" Dad inquired.

Jim hesitated for a minute and then replied, "I don't have a complete answer. But the first lesson I need to persistently implement, is always to pay much closer attention to the line of waiting customers—especially whenever it's getting longer, and the waiting time gets closer to the twenty minute mark."

"It's a novel thought," Dad said. "What then would be your next step?"

"With my persuasive charm I would try to make them wait a bit longer," Jim answered smiling, but quickly dismissed his solution. "It would probably buy me only a little more time."

"So what would you do, will you simply let them go?" Dad asked.

"Well... maybe I can be slightly unorthodox and offer them a special discount if they would agree to wait longer and dine the moment a table becomes available."

"It sounds like a good idea," Dad responded. But Jim, that in essence defies the expected response time rule," Didn't you say it shouldn't be longer than twenty minutes? How much longer would they be waiting before giving up—even with your discount?"

Jim sighed. "Maybe it will hold for a little bit longer. But you are right. It sounds like using a bandage instead of a real cure."

Steve, who was attentively listening to their conversation, added. "Your focus is on the waiting line. But what happens meanwhile with customers who are already seated? Are they receiving a prompt service while the restaurant is becoming full?"

Being bombarded with questions from Dad and Steve, Jim said, "I must find a way to seat them quickly and maintain a prompt service for all, even when we become very busy. Somehow I should flex things out, and...."

"That's it!" Steve excitedly cut Jim off in the middle of his explanation. "Jim just gave us the answer. Whenever the pressure of customer demand builds up, we must find a way to flex capacity—before service time begins to stretch out and sales opportunities slip away."

Dad looked at Steve and replied instinctively. "It may not be as simple as it sounds and also it can become too expensive. I would first resort to pushing out the waiting time."

"Even Jim said it will not hold for too long—like using a Band-Aid," Steve persisted. "I'm afraid that's exactly what too many people do, and eventually lose the customer and the sale. I think if you want to always be on top, you can't compromise the expected response time for your customer demand—it's like a contract you never want to breach."

Early Warning Light

There was a moment of silence and Jim, who was listening carefully to Dad and Steve, was ready to share his point of view. But he had to put it aside. A waitress just walked in, asking for an immediate help in the kitchen. "Gentlemen I'm afraid I have to leave, but it seems you are on track," he said.

He then looked at Dad and added, "It looks as if my role of pulling you out is over, and you can continue to roll on. I hope you send Steve home quickly before he falls asleep right here."

"But, Jim, before you leave, how would you go about flexing capacity?" Steve asked.

"I will seriously explore it once I have calculated my lost opportunities. I've got to try to implement the notion and see how it works," Jim said, and then left.

Lunch time had passed, and once again Dad and Steve were the only customers at the restaurant. Jim's employees were still busy cleaning up. Yet the noise around them didn't disrupt Dad and Steve from carrying on with their deep conversation.

Dad pushed his coffee cup aside and said, "Steve, I have to make a confession. I almost fell into the old habit trap and probably Jim did too. Our initial reaction was to push the customer out—hoping to buy a little more time."

He paused. "I guess extending the schedule is a natural reaction to pressure when your demand builds up. Maybe you can use a little leeway to reduce some of the impact. But it only buys you a short-term relief—and it bites real hard when eventually your customers have been pushed too far out. Therefore, to overcome the real problem, there is no choice but to flex out your capacity."

Appreciating Dad's openness Steve said, "So now that Jim has seen his cycles and got the lost opportunities notion, do you think he will implement any changes?"

"I guess if not, the only choice he has is to become a three-star Michelin graded restaurant," Dad said with a smile. "By being a high-end business he could afford pushing out his service time to weeks, if not months, and yet be full to capacity at all times. However, knowing Jim, he would easily lose all of the fun."

And Steve could imagine Jim wearing a chef's tall cap, cooking dinner with a sad face, while a long line of starving people salute a Michelin flag in front of his restaurant.

Steve's imaginary scene was interrupted by the ring of Dad's phone. Dad answered the call and it was Mr. Bupti on the line. "Hello, can you hear me?" Mr. Bupti asked. "It's very noisy here, I do apologize," he continued with his distinct accent. "Am I speaking to the owner? I am Mr. Bupti from the Bupti Service Company and I talked to your son last night. He said I can call you today. Is it a good time?"

Dad had hard time hearing Mr. Bupti. The hum of a large space mixed with loud announcements in the background, masked his voice. Yet he was curious enough to continue the call. "Yes I am the owner and we can carry on. In fact I am sitting here with my son, and he had told me all about your conversation." He then whispered to Steve, "It's him; Mr. Bupti is on the line."

"I am so sorry to interrupt," Mr. Bupti apologized. "I heard about your reputation through my relatives living in your area. I thought we can find some mutual interest in our businesses, and maybe we can work something out. In fact, I am right now waiting for a flight connection at London airport, and that's the reason for the loud noise. I will be seeing my relatives tomorrow, so maybe we can get together within a few days time?"

Dad hesitated for a minute.

"Hello, hello, are you still on the line?" Mr. Bupti asked.

"Well, I believe we can arrange a meeting soon," Dad replied. "Why don't you call after you have landed, and we will set up a time?"

"Thank you so much, and I will..." Mr. Bupti's voice was completely masked by the sound of a loud announcement. In a moment he was back. "I am sorry but that is the final boarding call, I really have to go and again I thank you very much."

Dad wished him a safe flight and ended the call.

"I couldn't hear him very well, but he will be in town tomorrow," Dad said to Steve.

Steve raised his eyebrows. "Is that pure coincidence, or is Mr. Bupti eventually going to meet with Mr. Stanley at the bank? Is he the guest from overseas? Maybe after all, my intuition wasn't wrong. Did he mention anything about our financial situation?"

"Not explicitly," Dad replied. "But I guess we will know very soon."

"So now we have two important meetings, and the one with Mr. Stanley is scheduled for tomorrow," Steve said. "We have very little time. I think we need to gather all that we have thus far and organize it in a reasonable manner—so we can show our plan to the bank."

He started collecting all the charts and notes that were lying on the table. "Here we have the key steps for our plan. We can explain our ten-year chart along with the others, tie everything together, and show our way to recovery for long term success." Steve then sighed. "Dad, I wish we had a little more time. I could have put it all in a nice presentation form to strengthen our case."

"You are right, but our time is very tight. We will have to compromise with what we have."

"So let's sort it all now," Steve replied.

"I agree, but before we do it there is one more thing we need to clear up," Dad said.

"What is it?" Steve asked.

"To have a better grasp on what capacity is and when to flex it out," Dad answered.

He held Jim's cycles chart and said, "Look, Steve, if we will continue plotting it for more weeks, I would be surprised if Jim's shift-to-shift erratic cycles would look different from what we have in front of us. So what is his capacity?"

"What do you mean by that, Dad? I thought he provided us with a good explanation."

"Not entirely," Dad said and pointed at Jim's chart. "As you said, for each marked point there is an untold story behind it. When Jim had twenty-eight customers on the first day's breakfast, it was well below his capacity to host. Then you see points of fifty and even fifty one. Does fifty one then, represent his capacity?"

Before Steve could respond he continued. "If you recall, he said that whenever he has forty customers a meal, he starts to feel the pressure—and possibly lose a customer. Beyond that, things begin to get real messy, where he struggles not to exceed his expected service time. I guess what I'm trying to say is that instead of a single number that defines your capacity, there is a range where service begins to slacken off."

"But that doesn't go hand in hand with what you learn in school," Steve insisted.

"Probably not," Dad responded. "All I am trying to suggest is that somewhere in the cycle, pressure builds up—and way before your capacity is maxed out, you are already losing business without realizing it."

Steve shook his head. "What you are suggesting Dad, is an entirely different concept."

"Maybe so!" Dad replied. "Instead of looking at your capacity as a singular point, it is a range. That's exactly what I mean."

Dad paused for a minute. "That's what happened to me back then with my bottleneck search. I did not realize early enough the wave of incoming customers' orders, and all my efforts were like chasing my own tail. We had already lost opportunities and a rising number of unhappy customers—who eventually jumped off the momentum wheel on its way downhill.

"Looking at it from where we are now, Steve, it is like I needed a red light, situated at the bottom of my capacity range, signaling when things were beginning to pile up, telling me I had better react immediately."

"So Dad...." Steve said, but Dad didn't let him interrupt.

Excitedly he said, "Anyone who runs a business must define its capacity and the pressure range. It is a key to avoid paying the price of lost opportunities and falling into the trap of chasing shifting bottlenecks, moving from one place to another."

"So, Dad," Steve said, this time without being cut short, "How do you make it work?"

Dad hesitated for a minute. "Well, I don't have it sorted out yet, but I could give it a try. First, you have to clearly define what your customers' expected service time is. It sounds simple, yet it may be more complicated than it looks. It took a whole discussion with Jim before we concluded his maximum would be around the fifteen- to twenty-minute mark—and you have to define it along the entire service cycle."

"It sounds like a good start," Steve responded. "So what would you say is our customers' expected response time?"

"Well, it depends on lot of things and..." Dad began answering but quickly dismissed the suggestion. "It would take too long to discuss it now. So please add it to our action list; and anyhow it would be better if we first talk to our customers in order to figure it out."

"It's an excellent idea. So where do you go next?"

"Once you figure your customers required service time, you have to wrestle with defining your capacity and its pressure range. At the bottom of the range you have to have a sort of alert mechanism, like an early warning light, to tell you where you are. That's the point where you must flex your capacity, before your response time begins to stretch out—which eventually could turn into a *bye* customers' situation."

Steve began to write down the key steps of the idea:

- Find what your customers' expected service time is
- Clearly define your capacity and its pressure range
- Establish an early warning mechanism for flexing capacity

"I can't wait implementing it." Steve said.

"Maybe we can try doing it with Jim's, as if were acting as his consultants," Dad responded. "It can help clarify what we need to do for ourselves. We already established with him his customers' required service time. He also said that whenever there are forty people dining, the pressure starts and service may begin to slacken off. That would be the lower pressure point. He can still seat more people, say, up to fifty or even more. So at forty, although being distant from the maximum seating capacity, he must flex his capacity. Reaching the forty people mark would be the warning signal for the entire staff to speed things up—making sure no customer would be waiting more than, say, ten minutes. Meanwhile, he should set up more tables, possibly add another person to the serving staff, and above all—he must closely monitor the buildup of customers waiting. Not having Jim with us, that is as far as I can go. But I'm sure he could have come up with even better solutions."

Dad then took his marker pen and drew on Jim's chart the capacity range concept and its early warning signal image.

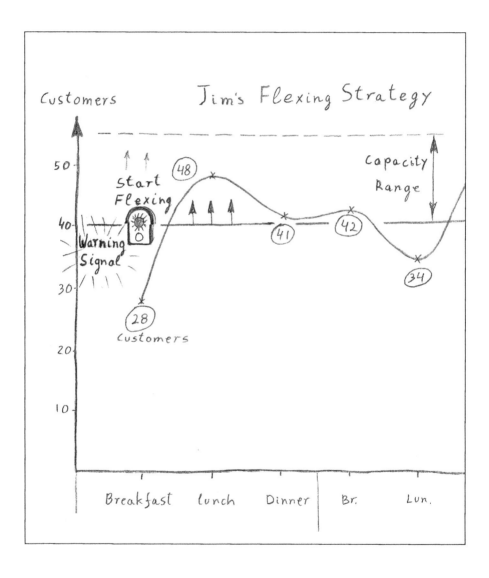

Steve examined the chart and said, "But Dad, there is still a major hurdle to overcome—the whole notion goes against most people's intuition. Don't we usually wait until our capacity is full and only then begin to react?"

"That is the vicious-cycle trap, but by then it is already too late," Dad said. He took a breath, "There are lots of ways to flex capacity once you open your mind—and it is important doing it early enough. I am sure that if anyone is challenged with this way of thinking, lots of good ideas will follow. In fact, I think I can come up with some good ideas for our business as well."

Dad stopped for a moment and then summed it up. "It all revolves around commitment to service and quick response time—and this applies to everyone. If you carefully think about it, the solution lies in flexing your capacity at the right time—and above all flexing your mind."

Cycles of Life and an Engagement Ring

3:00 p.m.

A hush had fallen over Jim's restaurant. The afternoon hours had settled in, and only Dad and Steve were sitting around the table. Jim's staff were finishing up their last duties inside of the kitchen and at the back office; ending their shift.

Dad looked at the grandfather clock, and this time he was not watching its pendulum. "Steve, it's getting late and we better wrap things up, especially if we want to give you some rest after a sleepless night and a long day." Their conversation was interrupted by a familiar voice from behind. "Hello gentlemen and excuse me for disrupting you. I was driving by and saw Dad's truck parked outside, so I assumed you were still here."

They turned around. "Janet, please have a seat and tell us, to what do we deserve the honor of seeing you again?" Dad said.

"Well... I'm here because you made me restless," Janet replied still standing. "You undeniably managed to challenge my mind. Since I left I was thinking about our discussion, and the charts you made. It definitely matched my intuition. So I tried to better understand your cycles' notion. I ran a lot of scenarios in my head, analyzing past and present. I looked at every aspect I could think of, and how I conduct my business. I think I found my bottleneck."

Simultaneously both Dad and Steve eagerly asked, "What is it, Janet?"

"Gentlemen, I'm not ready to so easily reveal my secrets," Janet answered jokingly. "Why don't you give it a try?"

"I think it is..." Dad started to answer, but noticing she was still standing he asked if she would join them.

Janet sat down and said, "Well I will save you the headache, so let me tell you what I have done. After I left, I had asked my accountant to prepare a chart of my monthly revenues over the last two years, so that I can see the picture of my business behavior over time. Isn't that what you suggested I do? You guys already created my *weekly* cycles chart with its volatile pattern—depicting my customers' service requirements and my workload, as it changes day by day."

Steve quickly found her chart, and Janet continued speaking while pointing at its peaks. "I thought about the weekend pressure buildup and the struggle to fulfill every customer requirement without pushing it too far out. And there are a few other things to think about. Doesn't that summarize your key concepts?"

"It does, Janet," said Dad, "but you still did not tell us what your bottleneck is."

"Regarding my bottleneck, it is not about what, but it is about whom," Janet replied. She saw the puzzled looks on Dad and Steve's faces and immediately clarified, "I have concluded that I am the bottleneck for my business."

She paused, and before they could interject she continued, "I realized that I spread myself too thin. While doing paper work and accounting data collection, I wasn't focusing as much as necessary on marketing. Being so busy serving customers, I didn't have enough time to think of how to improve my service. I wasn't able to accommodate adequately walk-in opportunities, and might have lost future customers. With the weekend pressure I often had to push customers too far out, and I am not sure what damage it might have caused. And the list goes on. I simply couldn't do most of the things I had in mind.

"And above all, I didn't take time away from the day to day pressure to simply think about my whole process—finding ways to make it more efficient. With that in mind, I came up with a few good ideas of how to offload some work off my shoulders and better serve my customers. Now I have to try them out, hopefully freeing myself from being the bottleneck—even with the random cycles."

Janet then candidly added, "I don't know about you gentlemen, but I have a feeling that being the bottleneck—as a business owner and a service provider—I am not there alone."

"But of course," Dad replied. After all he could definitely identify with Janet.

She then looked at them with a smile. "Now that my hidden secrets are revealed, may we talk about different kind of cycles?"

She paused as if she was waiting for a question to be asked.

Dad took the bait. "What other cycles are you talking about?"

"There are cycles of business, and there are cycles of life," Janet said. "We have already covered the business ones at depth, but we've barely touched on the other ones."

Dad and Steve looked at each other, trying to think what they might have left out in their model.

"Are you talking about the cycles of the economy?" Steve asked.

And Dad immediately added, "Are you referring to the recent recession and when we might get out?"

"No, gentlemen, your model is quite right," Janet answered. "But now that you have mentioned it, economy cycles might have been left out. I am sure we will find another opportunity to discuss this side as well."

She paused and then softened her tone. "With Steve's upcoming responsibilities heading the business, maybe he should move forward with his cycle of life."

Steve could tell where Janet was heading. "I got the hint and I already decided it's about time Sharon and I would get engaged. In fact I already know what ring Sharon would like."

Before Janet had a chance to react, a recognizable voice had joined in.

"Hello there, and Janet, what a pleasant surprise," Jim said.

"Hi, Jim, I haven't seen you in a while. How are you doing? I was here earlier, but you were not around," Janet said.

"Well, I'm just fine, but my head is still spinning from sitting with these two guys—not from drinking too much wine," Jim said with his big laugh. "I usually do that at the end of every day, just to keep my heart strong chasing around shifting bottlenecks."

"I am sure you got your share of cycles today, Jim," Janet laughed. "But hopefully Steve will take his next step in the cycle of life."

She then turned to Dad. "I got an idea. It would be nice if you go with Steve to buy Sharon the engagement ring."

"I wish I could join them, as I can be a good consultant," Jim said. "But I have to stay here to supervise the dinner shift."

Before things got completely out of hand, Dad was back in charge. "We can tie it altogether and meet here for dinner next week on Saturday night to celebrate Steve's new role heading our business—and surprise Sharon as well.

"I'm sure Jim will give us the best table, and he and his wife, Margaret, will be sitting with us also. Steve and I will arrange for Mom and Sharon to join us, and Janet, you and your daughter Caroline are invited too. Without a doubt, we all are going to enjoy a great meal, since I know Jim provides nothing but the best.

"Now, Steve, please get these people off my back, and let's go and get the ring. Then you can get some sleep so you can restore your energy for the challenges ahead. And let's all agree—no business and cycles talk during the dinner celebration."

As he was talking Dad's phone rang. He looked at the incoming call number on the screen and asked to be excused for a couple of minutes. He took a few steps aside. It was Amos calling in. "I have some good news. With the help of our close friends we managed to get you the money. I hope that it would get the bank immediately off your back. Let's meet as soon as possible so we can work out the arrangements."

Dad caught his breath. Excitedly he said, "I have no words for thanking you. Please pass it along. Your timing couldn't have been better. Tomorrow we have the meeting at the bank."

With a sigh of relief he added, "Can you also join us for a dinner next Saturday night? We have planned a special dinner for Sharon and Steve, and you will be one of our honored guests."

"I gladly accept your invitation," Amos said.

"So let's meet at Jim's place tomorrow morning at seven-thirty," Dad said.

"I will be there seven-thirty sharp," Amos replied and ended the call. "Things are really happening fast in this town," he mumbled.

A NEW BEGINNING

Steve's story was reaching its conclusion. It was initiated by his phone call one evening to my office, asking a peculiar question, and it turned into the whole story you just read. But a few things were left out.

So I asked, "Steve, as much as I would like to hear about what happened at your dinner get together, can you tell me first how was the meeting at the bank and how did it go with Mr. Stanley?"

Although it happened a while ago, Steve didn't hesitate. "The evening before the meeting I had a chance to rest a bit. I couldn't fall asleep, but a big hug from Sharon, a long hot shower, and some rest put me back on my feet. The next day Dad met Amos first thing in the morning and they made all the necessary arrangements. Dad's spirits were very high. He was all excited that the financial crunch had been lifted, but above all for the support of his close friends. As scheduled, we met with Mr. Stanley in the afternoon.

"He asked us to take a seat and said in a formal tone, 'I have known you for years and I have a high regard for your endeavor, but with the current situation the bank has some serious concerns.'

'Mr. Stanley, I believe we can resolve them all,' Dad responded. 'I wish we had a little more time to make a nice presentation, but instead we brought some information for you,' and Dad placed on the table his ten-year chart.

"Although Dad had the urge to tell Mr. Stanley that he doesn't need to worry—as the debt can be paid right away—we just carried on," Steve continued.

"We presented our insights and conclusions, along with our action plan. Mr. Stanley asked a few questions and said, 'I like what I see here and your analysis is fairly comprehensive. I appreciate your proposed implementation process, and it's rather unusual. Yet, I don't see here your projection of cash flow and it is important for extending your line of credit.'

Mr. Stanley paused. 'How soon can you get it to me? It is critical; there are decisions that must be made.'

'What about tomorrow?' Dad replied. 'We will work on it with top priority. After you reviewed it we can meet quarterly and examine how it meets real life.'

'It's a good idea,' Mr. Stanley replied. 'After I assess your projection I will be in touch.'

"Then," Steve continued as though he was reliving that moment, "Dad stood up and smiled. 'There is one more thing that will ease things a little,' and he handed a check covering the debt to Mr. Stanley.

"While shaking hands with Mr. Stanley Dad said, 'I insist you would review our plan and monitor its outcome. Steve will be happy to do business with you for a long time, as he is taking the company lead from now on.'

As Steve was finishing his recap of the meeting I said, "I can only imagine what was going through Mr. Stanley's head at that time; and by the way did you meet with him later on to review your cash projection?"

"Yes we did, and the fact that our debt was already paid off changed things altogether," Steve answered, waiting for the next question.

"Steve, thanks for sharing it and my curiosity is satisfied," I said. "Now let's get back to when all of you gathered for dinner. Can you tell me what happened there?"

Steve tone of voice lightened, as he was capturing the moments of a special evening. "We all met for dinner, and it had been a long time since I saw Mom and Dad so excited. The dinner turned into a real celebration. After all, it was a new beginning for all of us, in one way or another.

"Dad formally announced his upcoming retirement, and together with Mom they were looking forward to opening a new chapter in their lives. They decided the first trip they took would be to one of the Caribbean islands to enjoy cocktails, sun, sand, people watching and surfers catching waves," Steve said, amused.

He then added, "Regarding myself, I proposed to Sharon that night and a year later we got married. And... Oh yes, I almost forgot tell you about the other news. Amos, who sat next to Janet that evening, got up the courage to ask her out. They're still seeing each other. I guess his laid-back personality balances well with her vibrant character."

"Is that the end of the story or there is more to come?" I asked.

"Well, on the social side, that about sums it up. But there is more to tell," Steve said.

"Jim and I became close friends, frequently consulting with each other. Sharon eventually opened her own arts and crafts business. Jim managed to figure out his lost opportunities, and it turned out even bigger than what Dad and I had initially estimated based on his charts. His food was always well-known for its quality, but his ability to complement it with expeditious service whenever the pressure was on, allowed him to capture most of his lost opportunities and earn new customers.

"Janet, in her usual down-to-earth efficient manner, used her charts to analyze her business. She found ways to expand her service capacity, flexing it up and down according to her weekly cycles. It has allowed her to improve her response time for her customers and to better accommodate random walk-in's. She managed to relieved some of her personal pressure, especially at peak times—all yielding more business and success."

Steve stopped for a minute as if he was trying to see if anything was left out, and then added, "Maybe not any less important is our monthly get-together. All of us have decided to meet on a regular basis to share our problems and gained experiences. We try to help each other, even though we all provide different types of service. We are even thinking about adding a few more friends to our monthly meeting group."

"What about your business, Steve—what did you do there?" I asked eagerly.

"After the dinner excitement had subsided, and the meeting with the bank was behind us, there were a lot of things left to internalize. Dad and I set aside hours to develop further all of the insights we had acquired, and transformed them into actions. It was not done in a single day. Rather, it turned into a gradual process of deepening our understanding of the way we run our business.

"One of the most important lessons I learned, was to always take the customer view. It wasn't easy to switch roles from the service provider point of view, but it paid off. I took it as a basis for everything."

"Before you go on, Steve, can you be more specific?" I interjected.

"By looking at my personal experience as a customer, I learned how delicate and fragile the interaction with the service provider can be. I realized how quickly a *buy* customer can turn into a *bye* one. I also realized that as a service provider, there is so much you can do to prevent such situations from happening."

"And is there anything else the customer can do before walking away?" I asked.

Steve took a minute. "I think it is always the responsibility of the service provider. As a customer, I suppose if you care for the service you would like to receive, you could communicate your dissatisfaction at the very early stage. It can give you and the service provider an opportunity to work things out. Any later than that could make the customer feel bad enough to simply walk away—and even worse, to never come back."

"Steve, you have summed it all up really well. So what happened then?" I continued.

"I had sat with Dad for hours to get our customers' DNA knowledge right off his head. We started implementing it with our top three customers, using a simple information format, and then continued to cover them all. We also plotted our process and developed a way to monitor our service ratio efficiency.

"Then we moved on to deal with bottlenecks and cycles," Steve continued. "And Dad was right. The cycles of our customers' demand were not less erratic than Jim's. By putting them together with Dad's ten-year chart, we got a real understanding of our business.

"We then talked to our customers and defined their required response time, and developed a method to identify when service starts to slacken off. We analyzed our service capabilities, realized our true capacity, and we established our *red light* mechanism at about twenty five percent below the max. So whenever our customers' demand accumulated high enough, we were able to flex capacity up—keeping our quick response to every customer's request."

He paused. "And not less important, maintain our quick and high quality service even when business had slowed down. You know, you can always have a last minute call for an urgent service, or a walk in situation. If you don't rapidly accommodate the request, you can easily lose a customer. It all allowed us to capture lost opportunities and reduce *bye* customers to nil."

Steve sighed as if he was re-living all of the hard work he had done. "All these actions have lead to constantly increasing our customer base. Coupled with our continued investment in technical capabilities and craftsmanship, we have elevated our reputation to one of the best around. Now we're a leader in our service industry.

"We extended our business beyond our county to reach the whole state, and recently we have expanded our service to other states—in fact, to the entire region."

Steve paused as if he was giving me time to fully appreciate his accomplishments.

"It is definitely a great achievement, and I'm sure it improved your bottom line performance as well?" I said.

"Yes, it did," Steve responded. "As we expanded our customers' base and improved our service efficiencies, our profit increased accordingly."

"That sounds terrific, Steve, and it looks that you have just described a methodology that anyone can utilize—in all walks of life," I responded. "Does it sum it all up?"

"Not quite," he responded. "Didn't you forget something?"

It took me a minute. "Oh yes, what about Mr. Bupti, did you eventually meet?"

"He called Dad after our meeting with the bank," Steve said. "It wasn't long after he had landed and visited his relatives in town. We met him two days later. Until now I don't know if he was the guest Mr. Stanley was expecting, or was it a pure coincidence. But with the way things took their turn, it didn't really matter."

"Can you clarify?" I asked. "Did he not express a strong interest in your business?"

"Yes he did, even more then we imagined," Steve responded. He then paused. "If initially he presented a threat for taking over, with Amos and our friends' financial help, it entirely changed the situation."

"So did he just took off and disappeared? I asked.

Steve laughed and said, "Quite the contrary. From a potential foe he turned to be a real friend and a partner. Having the financial burden lifted off, it put the entire interaction with him on a new platform. It allowed us to explore mutual interests instead. His company offered services in their Continent, and we came to a conclusion that we can benefit together by collaborating. We ended up representing each other's interests. He benefited from our experience in quality and technology, and we, from adding new services to our market. It really worked well.

"It's a real surprise and I wish you the best," I replied. "I hope that many situations would end like the way yours did. So I assume it brings us to the end of your story?"

"Not yet," Steve said. "One day I was looking back at how it had all begun, with Dad turning over his business to me, and how far we have come since—and a new idea just crossed my mind. I asked myself, if we know how to fix tools, why can't we make them? I presented the idea to Mr. Bupti and together we opened a manufacturing facility, which I run in addition to the service facility."

"It's a great idea, Steve—to be a key service provider and a manufacturer as well is very unique. You already had one beginning in taking over your Dad's service endeavor, and now it sounds like another new beginning. It must be exciting."

"It definitely is, but it brought whole new challenges that I did not expect. With the knowledge I acquired, coupled with experience, I was convinced it would be similar to our service enterprise. But it was not.

"Frustrated, I tried to re-examine what I was doing wrong, and I realized that running our new endeavor was a whole new ball game. I decided to go back to the basics, and that's what made me call you."

"I am not sure I understand," I responded.

"Your article 'On Cycles and Bottlenecks,' prompted my call which made me tell you the whole story," Steve said. "I found it on Dad's desk late at night after he surprised me with his retirement decision."

He stopped for a moment. "At first the article was rather confusing, but eventually it served as a catalyst for Dad and I to ask questions and struggle with unfamiliar concepts. We presented them to Janet and Jim, and later on to a few more friends. Struggling together helped us in figuring out some missing elements. Finally we came up with the course of action we needed to take."

He then sighed. "We came a long way and it worked well with our service endeavor, but I feel that in our new facility I'm stuck."

I took me a minute to reply. "Based on your fascinating and elaborate story, Steve, you seem to have graduated successfully from the *intuitive phase* and moved into the *quantitative phase*. Perhaps you are ready for the next one—the *scientific phase*."

"I'm not sure what you mean by that," Steve said.

"Looking at the evolution of almost every business, it usually starts with the intuitive stage," I said. "The enterprise is relatively small and as an owner and manager, you know basically almost everything that's going on. You are focused on establishing your trade and developing a sufficient customer base. Craftsmanship, quality, and salesmanship are at the top of your list. This phase is extremely challenging since you must excel in all of these areas to survive and eventually establish yourself. The day-to-day decision making is done primarily by intuition and is usually sufficient to carry you on.

"But there comes a point where all of a sudden you may face pressure you never experienced before. You have more customers, each with their special requirements. You may have added more personnel, and your workload begins to creep up on you. At this stage not only do you have more to deal with, but managing by intuition is far from sufficient and things start to slip away. Didn't you Steve, refer to it using your blindfolded captain analogy?"

"Yes I did," Steve responded. "So was that the stage we were at when Dad decided to hand me over his responsibilities?"

"It seems that way," I replied. "And if I may add, it is a critical point where many people falter. If you don't find a way to shift to another level it will set you back. Too often your endeavor becomes mediocre and stagnant—where you may stay where you are—sometimes for the rest of your life. And if you are not careful, it may turn into a complete fall.

"Your father was fortunate enough to avoid the fall. But wasn't he facing a wall, every time he regained energy—only to face another vicious cycle? It was exactly the stage your father was at in the beginning of your story, Steve—with a Sisyphean struggle of rise and fall throughout his business cycles."

"So what had prompted the change?" Steve asked.

"The change of circumstances," I replied. "All of a sudden you were faced with a new responsibility of taking over, and on top of that you had your issues with the bank and Mr. Bupti pushing from behind. Just look what you accomplished in only one night and a day. You analyzed your process using logic and charts. You developed an improvement plan and understood your customer side. You plotted cycles, realized capacity and how to flex it out. That and more, all turned your intuition into a quantitative and measurable form. You had elevated yourself from the *intuitive* to the *quantitative phase*. That is what you discovered, Steve, in turning your service enterprise around.

"That's a good observation," Steve said. "So using all of it in our manufacturing facility, why do I feel it's not enough?"

"Maybe because you are faced with a new reality and complexities," I answered. "But with your gained experience, you could move into the *scientific phase* to crack the puzzle of running your new facility—and it will allow you to break new boundaries in your service enterprise as well."

Steve was silent for a minute and then said, "That sounds good, so how do we start?"

"As a start, I have one question you should answer without putting it aside because of the day-to-day pressure—and you must not let any recent crisis cloud your mind."

"So what is that question?" Steve asked.

"What is your *real* bottleneck?"

www.cyclesofintuition.com

Author Biography

I. Kostika, business consultant, educator and author, is the creator and leading exponent of Flow Management Technology (FMT). His pragmatic approach to engineering and understanding of scientific concepts, coupled with his extensive business experience, has been instrumental in developing this visionary science based technology. In 1987 Mr. Kostika founded his business consulting and education company, in Milford, Connecticut.

Mr. Kostika is the author of the book "Breaking Out of the Box". Articles about his methodology and its implementations in leading companies in the USA were published in professional magazines. He was a featured monthly columnist for Tooling & Production Magazine. He also developed ManuFlow, a software simulation educational tool. He was invited as a keynote speaker at several professional associations, and made presentations at academic institutions such as Yale University, where some utilized his ideas and simulation software for teaching.

His methodology has been implemented in a wide range of companies large and small, including Caterpillar, Goodyear Tire and Rubber, Black & Decker, TRW and many more.

Prior to forming his own company, Mr. Kostika worked many years for Dr. Goldratt, the author of the bestseller book "The Goal" and developer of the Theory of Constraints (TOC).

Mr Kostika holds degrees in Mechanical, Industrial and Management Engineering. He has served on the Board of Directors of various companies. In addition to his consulting activities, he is an active partner of manufacturing and service companies.

Mr. Kostika resides in Connecticut, USA, and is an enthusiastic tennis player and sports fan.

For more information visit www.cyclesofintuition.com

Made in the USA
Las Vegas, NV
27 March 2021